COMING OF AGE

COMING OF AGE

Navigating Parish Pastoral Council Responsibilities

A Benedictine Perspective

Justin Harkin

VERITAS

Published 2021 by
Veritas Publications
7–8 Lower Abbey Street
Dublin 1
Ireland
www.veritas.ie

ISBN 978 1 84730 989 1

10 9 8 7 6 5 4 3 2 1

A catalogue record for this book is available from the British Library.

Designed by Jeannie Swan, Veritas Publications
Printed in the Republic of Ireland by SPRINT-print Ltd, Dublin

Veritas books are printed on paper made from the wood pulp of
managed forests. For every tree felled, at least one tree is planted,
thereby renewing natural resources.

In memory of my father
and
in gratitude to my mother

For Pobal Dé
especially of
the Dioceses of Elphin, Clonfert and Tuam

Contents

Foreword

I very much welcome this interesting reflection on the mission of Parish Pastoral Councils in the light of Benedictine Spirituality. The author, Justin Harkin, has given many years of service in the Diocese of Elphin in the area of Pastoral Development and Faith Formation.

The best books are not the ones that simply provide information, but the ones that encourage reflection and imagination. It had never really crossed my mind before that the monastic spirituality of St Benedict might have something to contribute to the understanding of Parish Pastoral Councils (PPC). Parishes, while they are not monastic, are called to be communities of disciples, where the faith of each is nourished by the faith of the community.

Fifteen years ago, I was appointed parish priest of Glendalough, a place that is well known for its monastic history. It was my first time to have responsibility for a parish and I knew that I had a lot of things to learn. I suspect that the parishioners also realised very quickly that I had a lot to learn. Nobody has all the answers or all the gifts, and that includes the priest. One of the great blessings of that time was the process of discernment which led to the development of a very diverse but vibrant PPC.

The parish council can never be just about a few good people 'helping Father with his work'. It is about developing a shared vision and a shared responsibility for the mission of the parish. I am also a firm believer in the distinction between the PPC and the Parish Finance Council. This is because if finance and the maintenance of buildings becomes the preoccupation of the PPC, it has a way of sucking up all the energy and the pastoral needs of the community will often be relegated to the background.

St Luke tells us that, as the shepherds returned to their flocks after the Nativity and the choirs of angels withdrew, 'Mary pondered these things in her heart' (Lk 2). The *Lectio Divina* approach to prayer is very central to Benedictine Spirituality and it begins with listening attentively to God's word, reflecting on it and then allowing our prayer and our action to flow from what we have heard. As Justin comments, in chapter three, this attentive listening with the heart is essential to any form of community and to the development of a shared vision which is rooted in faith. A PPC is called to be a listening community; listening to what God is saying; listening to what the parishioners are saying and, of course, listening to one another.

Attentive listening is not a skill that comes naturally to everybody or to every group and, for that reason, I believe that formation and ongoing reflection must be part of the life of every PPC. In a busy world, the urgency of 'getting things done' sometimes persuades us that we have no time for reflection. Without attentive listening and prayerful reflection, however, it is difficult to know if what we are doing is really for the good of the community or in accordance with the mind of God. In drawing attention to this, Justin does an important service.

Towards the end of the book, there is a chapter entitled 'Coming of Age: Where to From Here?' The title suggests to me two very important dimensions of the mission of the PPC. One is the joy of realising that, after some time working together, we have matured in our own vision of parish and in our capacity to offer leadership. The second is that realisation that often comes as we climb a mountain; when it dawns on us that this is not actually the summit; that there is still further to go. As Justin comments, Pastoral Council members are at their best when 'they embody a missionary spirit ever willing to support initiatives that help others grow in faith'. The energy to go further is an essential part of the process of discerning when it is good for someone to remain on a PPC for another term and when it is time for him or her to move on to some other aspect of mission.

Stability in the Benedictine tradition is associated with being rooted in a particular community. It is about committing myself to that community, with all its human imperfections, rather than looking for paradise on earth, which is only an illusion. But it is helpful to remember that rootedness is for growth. In the life of any parish community there are two extremes to be avoided. One extreme is the lack of continuity and the other is the lack of growth. St Peter writing to Christians in Asia Minor, in the first century AD, said: 'you also, like living stones, are being built into a spiritual house' (1 Pt 2:5). Christian community is built on the spiritual legacy of generations of people who have lived, worked, prayed and played in a particular place. It is organic. The reality of Christian community is not carved in stone, or captured in buildings, or confined by geographical boundaries.

Lectio Divina invites us to reflect on what the Word of God is saying to us in the concrete reality of our own circumstances today, and not just in the pages of a book, even the Bible. Similarly, while consolidating what has been achieved, a PPC must always be asking, what is God calling us to be and to do today, in our parish and in communion with other parishes and the wider Church. To that extent, the PPC, through its own dialogue and in all its activity, should bear witness to the kind of missionary discipleship to which every Christian is called.

I hope that this book, as it brings the insights of Benedictine Spirituality face to face with the challenges of pastoral leadership, will help many Parish Pastoral Councils to move beyond a pragmatic agenda-driven way of working, to the development of a shared vision for parish and a capacity to inspire others with that vision.

+ *Kevin Doran*
Bishop of Elphin

Acknowledgements

This book would not have been possible without the trust and goodwill of the clergy and laity of the Elphin diocese. I am grateful to Bishop Kevin Doran for providing the Foreword and to the many women and men, laity, religious and clergy, who presented for courses and workshops over the past twenty years, especially those who voiced their aspirations, questions, concerns and stories.

In coming into this work and for more than a decade I benefitted from the support of the Elphin Diocese's Pastoral Planning Group and today I enjoy the support of the diocese's recently established Parish Pastoral Council Team. I am grateful to all who served on the latter body, particularly Fr Ciaran Whitney, and to those who now support programme development and delivery.

I also acknowledge with deep affection and gratitude my brother David who kindly proof read earlier drafts of all chapters. I am very grateful to him and to Fr Columba McCann OSB, Glenstal Abbey, for their encouragement and pertinent editorial suggestions. Fr Columba's willingness to share from his own lived experience of parish ministry and Benedictine Spirituality was also hugely helpful and has added greatly to this book.

My wife, Fiona, and children, Eimear and Conor, have also been a great support, not least in sharing me with the writing process. Thank you! The prayer support of the Benedictine community of Glenstal Abbey – monks and oblates – is also gratefully appreciated, not just in relation to this initiative but on an ongoing basis.

Finally, my thanks to Veritas for their willingness to publish this book.

Proceeds from the sale of this book will be used to support the building and resourcing of St John Bosco Academy, St Patrick's Parish, Zing, Diocese of Jalingo, Nigeria. For more information about this project see: www.creideamh.ie/mission-project.

Introduction

This book has been written for all who serve on Parish Pastoral Councils. It has been written particularly for women and men who exert a service of leadership, or who feel called to exert such a service in a spirit of co-responsibility with others. It recognises that though the need for such bodies has never been greater, members can periodically find themselves grappling with questions of identity, meaning and purposefulness. It treats this recognition as a stage of personal and group spiritual growth, rich in potential for Parish Pastoral Council members and their parish communities.

When it comes to serving on a Parish Pastoral Council, a member's starting point is always their own Christian identity. Over the past two millennia many Christian spiritualities have emerged, all the fruit of individual and group efforts to pursue the Christian life. One of the most enduring is Benedictine Spirituality. It dates back to the sixth century when c. AD 520 St Benedict of Nursia wrote a monastic rule that continues to be lived by Benedictine, Cistercian, Trappist and Camaldolese communities today. Consisting of a prologue and seventy-three chapters, ranging from a few lines to several pages, this Rule reflects St Benedict's own experience as a Christian, monk and leader, and his study of Christian writings of the time.

Although written for monks and nuns, time has revealed the applicability of St Benedict's Rule to Christian living in every era and culture. The Rule contains pointers all Christians can embrace, particularly regarding values such as patience, simplicity, time for prayer, humility, caring for others and living in community. It touches on matters that concern all of us and illuminates how to live generously and wisely. Through it many lay women and men have found a way of entering a more simple, balanced and prayerful Gospel-centred life, as well as a means of enriching their varied commitments and responsibilities.

When we are good enough to commit to a Parish Pastoral Council, parish project or initiative we like to see it realise positive outcomes for others as well as ourselves. The purpose of this book is to help Parish Pastoral Council members to re-explore their involvement by drawing on the timeless wisdom and vitality of St Benedict's insights and encouragement. In this way it hopes to help you and others realise more of your council's potential.

We are forever members of a Church in transition. Parish Pastoral Councils are now being invited to play a pivotal role in the current transition, i.e. of supporting fellow parishioners to partake more fully in the ministerial dimensions of parish life. As lay persons, we shall never replace our priests or their ministry but there is more we can do and possibly need to do if our parishes are to thrive as faith communities. We are people with a rich faith heritage, one many of us desire to share with future generations. Many of us are also very busy people, constantly juggling commitments. Each day, week and year we must prioritise. By committing to a fixed-term with our Parish Pastoral Council, we have included the preservation, well-being and future of the faith communities that comprise our parish among our priorities. Undertaken in the correct spirit this can be both life-giving and onerous. There is much to navigate and negotiate if we are to exercise this service meaningfully and fruitfully.

This book does not set out to inform you how to plan or run a Parish Pastoral Council meeting or facilitate a parish-wide consultation. Such resources already exist.[1] It doesn't set out to revise the vision underpinning Parish Pastoral Councils. Rather it seeks to explore the personal and group challenges presented by that vision. To support your engagement, I have used a number of real-life stories from my and others' pastoral experience. In every instance the details have been changed to preserve the anonymity of those who feature. I have also followed the lead of Benedictine Spirituality writer Sr Joan Chittister OSB, and others, in editing St

Benedict's Rule to read in universal language. This is justified by the fact that the Rule has guided the lives of both women and men since its inception. Readers will also encounter references to sacred scripture in every chapter. These have been included to support those who wish to break their reading with moments of prayer. Where a quotation from sacred scripture is given, it has been taken from *The Jerusalem Bible*, with the exception of quotations from the psalms, which are taken from *The Psalms: The Grail Translation – Inclusive Language Version* (London: HarperCollins, 1995).

Chapter one shares how I came to connect the wisdom of Benedictine Spirituality with Parish Pastoral Council membership. In chapter two, I introduce oblature, a form of Benedictine Spirituality lived by lay women and men and some secular clergy, as a premise to explore Pastoral Council membership. Here particular attention is given to exploring the dispositions of our hearts. Chapters three, four and five follow by exploring three Benedictine dispositions that can be applied to all Pastoral Council service, *obedientia* (obedience), *stabilitas* (stability) and *conversatio morum* (daily attentiveness to conversion of heart, permanently striving to improve one's attitude and participation in community life as an expression of one's desire for union with God). My underlining aspiration here is to name and address issues that we may need to tend to if we are to embrace the call to mission so central to our faith.

In chapter six my gaze turns to leadership and authority, individual and collective, i.e. in light of the vision underpinning the work of Pastoral Councils and considerations that support good pastoral outcomes.

Chapter seven is the heart of this book. It looks at how humility can help us to advance Evangelical Catholicism via pastoral initiatives in our parishes (these terms are explained in the chapter). Chapter eight also delves into the mission of every Parish Pastoral Council, drawing on personal encounters, recent

Vatican documents and other relevant experiences. Chapter nine, as well as recapping on salient inclusions in each chapter, stresses the importance of progressing in ways that are healthy and mindful that our service is a sharing in God's endeavour over and above anything of our own design or doing.

As a book it may be read privately or with a view to group discussion.

I hope that Parish Pastoral Council members who feel a degree of isolation or frustration at this time will find the book heartening and a support in contributing to the effectiveness of their council. This is a particularly challenging moment for the prophets among us, those whom the Holy Spirit is igniting by way of engaging the rest of us. If you are among them – and don't be surprised that you are – may you find a blessing in these pages.

Note

1   For example, Donal Harrington, *Tomorrow's Parish: A Vision and a Path*, Dublin: Columba Press, 2018 (revised edition), and Irish Catholic Bishops' Conference, *Living Communion: Vision and Practice for Parish Pastoral Councils Today*, Dublin: Veritas, 2011.

Chapter One

Seeking to Be Good at What We Do

Let faithful love and constancy never leave you: tie them around your neck, write them on the tablet of your heart. Thus you will find favour and success in the sight of God and of people

(Prov 3:3–4)

Seeking his workman in a multitude of people, the Lord calls out to him and lifts his voice again: Is there anyone here who yearns for life and desires to see good days?

(Ps 33[34]:13; RB, Prologue, 14–15)

❧ The mobile vibrates. It's Francis and I'm happy to take the call. 'How are you Francis?' I enquire. 'Caught for time Justin. Can Maura and I meet with you for coffee next time you are in our area?' We agree a date, time and venue and before Francis terminates the call I say, 'Mind if I ask what you want to chat about?' 'Sure. The Pastoral Council has asked Maura to serve as chairperson and me to serve as secretary. We're committed to our faith but this isn't our scene. We've a lot of reservations and can't see it working out. Maura's busy with work and family and doesn't feel she has the headspace. Tommy, her husband, is also very busy and she feels she needs to prioritise their children. I have less commitments but I can't see a relationship of trust evolving with Fr Marcus. The outgoing council has gone round in circles. It's hard to be enthusiastic.' I thank Francis for his candour and joke with him that the coffees will be on the bishop. Experience has taught me the importance of humour in sacred moments like this one. I am also deeply grateful for the call. My assessment is that Maura, Francis and Fr Marcus could offer excellent leadership within the council and parish, and that Francis' intuition about the centrality of trust to valuable outcomes from their time together is spot on. ❧

It is thirty-seven years (1983) since Pope John Paul II signed an apostolic constitution introducing a 'new' Code of Canon Law in the Roman Catholic Church. This Code drew its origin from a desire felt by Pope John XXIII (1958–1963) and others to support the renewal of Christian life throughout the world. The purpose of the Code was not to replace faith, grace, charisms (gifts given by the Holy Spirit for the building up of the Church) or charity in our lives as followers of Christ but to look towards 'the achievement of order' within our Church, 'such that while attributing a primacy of love, grace and the charisms, it facilitates at the same time an orderly development' in the life of the Church and in the lives of those of us who belong to it.[1] In honouring this purpose the 'new' Code sought to complement the teaching of the Second Vatican Ecumenical Council (1962–1965), which had been convened by John XXIII 'to promote the growth of the Catholic faith and a salutary renewal of morals among Christian peoples, to bring ecclesiastical (Church) discipline up to date, according to the needs of our times'.[2]

One of the striking inclusions in this Code were canons (laws) which spoke to the emerging awareness of the need for new degrees of partnership between clergy and laity, and the Code's suggestions as to how these might be structured and facilitated. For example, at diocesan level, bishops were now permitted to summon diocesan synods of selected clergy, religious and laity to assist them in discerning how best to respond to prevailing pastoral challenges.[3] It also allowed for the establishment of advisory Diocesan Pastoral Councils[4] that would include lay people[5] 'to study and weigh those matters which concern the pastoral works in the diocese, and to propose practical conclusions concerning them'. It also allowed for the establishment of Parish Pastoral Councils, parish bodies presided over by parish priests that would 'give help in fostering pastoral action.'[6] In so doing the Code recognised that partnership, if it were to be effective, must be structured and facilitated, and that consequent relationships, like all others, would need to be 'worked at'.

For twenty years it has been my privilege to support the formation and ongoing formation of Parish Pastoral Councils in the Diocese of Elphin in the West of Ireland. I have also sat with and at the feet of many people, clergy, religious and laity who have exercised a leadership role in a Church apostolic group. In that time I have witnessed Pastoral Councils thrive and collapse, rise and fall and rise again, either rejuvenate regularly or not at all, establish vibrant working relationships with their priest or lay members and other committed parishioners or never attain a satisfactory degree of mutual respect and care.

On occasion, when we have established a rapport of trust, I have invited members to communicate what motivates them to renew their commitment month after month. It's an important enquiry, frequently illuminating God's presence in their lives. When participants can name what they find life-giving about being involved we have much to be thankful for and to work on. When they don't, it is never because of a lack of goodwill. Invariably we begin to explore questions like 'Is there a value to a parish having a Pastoral Council?' and 'What are you hearing in this discussion that energises you?'

A number of the Psalms speak of the Israelites wandering in the dessert for forty years, 'finding no way to a city they could dwell in' (Ps 106:4). There are occasions when our involvement in Church activities can feel a bit like that. We can feel that we are not going anywhere, that what was once a source of curiosity and excitement has become mundane and uninteresting. We can find ourselves empathising with one another that we appear to be making little progress.

This brings me to the two quotations that opened this introduction. The first, from the Book of Proverbs, is my prayer for every reader of this book. The second alludes to my conviction regarding the place every Parish Pastoral Council member has in God's plan at this time. It's unlikely that you would have dipped into or begun to read these pages had the faithful love of God and neighbour not found a home in you. Your willingness to serve or to consider serving in a faith leadership group is not without foundation.

One of the interesting aspects of Parish Pastoral Councils is that members do not self-select. Rather other parishioners or clergy nominate them owing to something they recognise or see in them, something holy and significant, and pertinent to the ministry of the Church at this time. Your experience or intuition may also be telling you that acceptance of this ministry is not without inherent challenges. If that's the case, take heart. As the proverb communicates, through our faithful love and constancy we find favour and success in the sight of God and people.

The second quotation is from a less known source, a monastic rule committed to writing by St Benedict in the sixth century. In this particular sentence Benedict is speaking about God, drawing on a question found in Psalm 33: 'Seeking workers in a multitude of people, the Lord calls out to them and lifts his voice again: Is there anyone here who yearns for life and desires to see good days?' The message is very clear. When God decides to recruit, where does He go? He turns to those who yearn for life and who desire to see good days, not just for themselves but for others too!

If you currently serve with your Parish Pastoral Council or have been invited to join, you will know that it entails a commitment to a monthly meeting, and on occasion, a commitment to advancing a project or two between meetings. During your training you will most likely have received a definition of what the council is, emphasising that it is a leadership and consultative body that works in close partnership with the clergy of the parish to further the mission of Christ and His Church in the parish. If your council's up and running then you are likely to have participated in discussions pertaining to a whole myriad of Church activities – sacramental preparation, the quality of the Sunday Mass and timetabling of Masses, the parish mission, adult religious education, outreach to the marginalised, youth ministry, parish communications and celebrations, care of the elderly, care of the earth, welcoming the stranger and much more. Hopefully your experience has been and will continue to be life-giving for you, the other members and the parish … but that's not always the case. Like all groups comprising people there can be differences of opinion, interpersonal challenges, misunderstandings and a lingering doubt as to whether our efforts are fruitful.

From time to time we can all feel stressed, overburdened, anxious, fearful or a myriad of other feelings that detract from our happiness. That's human and natural and often there is just cause. The deeper reality, however, is that God desires our happiness and well-being and is forever inviting us to be a blessing in the lives of others. The desire to be happy is innate to all of us and readily integrates with a healthy Christian spirituality. Many of us know from experience the truth of St Francis' great prayer, that in giving we receive, that in bringing joy to others we do something just as wholesome for ourselves. If I were to invite you to think about something you continue to be grateful for from a previous community commitment you undertook I bet your list would include at least one enduring positive outcome. If I followed up by inviting you to name a regrettable group experience, you could probably do that too. Equally if I were to invite you to name what you had learned from that experience, I anticipate you would have a gem to share.

Recently I had occasion to reflect on some of my own experiences with pastoral groups that I am a member of. In doing so I became particularly appreciative of the women and men who exercised leadership with and for us. To use a local colloquialism, the fact that 'they had their act together' helped all of us to contribute and to feel good about our participation. Secondly, as a person somewhat disposed toward anxiety, I noted that I consistently feel more secure and content when a group remained welcoming and inclusive.

I have also known times of deep discomfort and spiritual restlessness and that has been harder to reflect on. Sometimes it was because I was railing internally against viewpoints and perspectives with which I totally disagreed. Other times, it was linked to a sense of futility, of our time not leading toward any valuable outcome for ourselves or others. Over time I have learned that it is a great blessing when adults can be truly authentic with one another and when there is scope for all to explore their hopes and fears, aspirations and concerns. The light of enthusiasm and conviction burns more brightly when that is the way.

All of us aspire to be happy and to be good at what we do. Some of us have developed ways of reviewing how we are getting along. I am among those who tend to reflect as I take an evening walk or peruse the shelves of a second-hand bookshop. Over time I have become more conscious of how time on my own nurtures my commitment to community projects and parish ministries. Not everything is enjoyable and nor does it need to be. Many women and men undertake ministries purely because it is the right thing to do. The fact that the joy of involvement can be short-lived doesn't deter us. At other times we recognise the need to pull back as marriage, family and employment commitments require more time. St John's reminder that God wants each of us to get beyond our fears[7] resonates deeply with me as I consider the relationship of life and ministry for many people I know. Another consideration is 'confidence'.

Confidence, consolidated by faith and good discernment, is, in my experience, a fruit of ongoing learning and conviction. It enables us to accept new opportunities and challenges – for example, serving as chairperson or secretary of one's Parish Pastoral Council – even when we have concerns about our inadequacies. We do well to remember St Paul's teaching that 'God did not give us a spirit of timidity, but the Spirit of power and love and self-control' and that we, women and men of faith, are never to be ashamed of witnessing to our Lord, or ashamed of those who are his prisoners, but rather share in their hardships for the sake of the Gospel (1 Tm 1:7–8). It's this same Spirit that desires to work through all of us for the sake of the Kingdom.

Some years ago I and others were invited to take leadership roles with an apostolic group that was really struggling. With the group we quickly faced a moment of decision – to give more time and energy to our mission or to walk away. The learning that followed was immense. We returned to the founding intention that had inspired past members and then began to clarify our expectations of ourselves. This helped us regain our focus and to see more clearly how we could achieve something of value for others as well as ourselves. Our secretary insisted that every meeting have an agenda and a new form of minute-taking, one more supportive of continuity. I didn't realise it at the time but this was our first step to accountability. With time the whole experience was to have a profound impact on my work with and for Parish Pastoral Councils. I came to appreciate that though the Church has offered us a new framework for working together we benefit in growing in our understanding of why we need to.

Around that time two other blessings also came my way. Firstly, I was invited to facilitate two dynamic Parish Pastoral Councils undertake a review of their experiences and to support them to discern priorities for the coming year. Both councils were characterised by a heart-warming positivity. I came to appreciate this was borne of graces acted upon by leaders and members. Both groups had a vision of what they were about and tended to be very good humoured with one another. They also manifested a certain liberty in so far as no one took themselves too seriously. Members were present because they wanted to be and readily saw, through the good work of their officers, the contribution they were making. They looked forward to their time together and to contributing to parish life.

Then and now it was and is my custom to participate in our parish's daily celebration of the Eucharist. Like other participants, I desire to be open to God's word through the readings. Around this time this was a real struggle and I happened to mention this to a priest friend. 'Well,' he said, 'what do you hear when you go to Mass?' I shared that Fr John was presiding these mornings and that my curiosity was sparked by a phrase toward the end of Eucharistic Prayer No. 1: 'graciously accept this oblation of our service'. My priest friend smiled. 'That's your prayer Justin. God is inviting you to ponder those words. Discuss them with him. That is his word to you!'

Within an hour I was preoccupied with responsibilities and thought no more about our conversation. Then, some months later, I found myself with a half hour to spare before a Dublin city centre meeting. There were two second-hand bookshops en route and within minutes I was perusing book spines, dull and glossy, pristine and showing the signs of use, until … well, what about that, a book entitled *The Oblate Life!*[8]

My post-meeting homeward train journey revealed a book expertly edited by a British Benedictine monk, Gervase Holdaway OSB. In it thirty-five writers, some Catholic, some of other Christian denominations, some clergy, others religious and others lay persons, some well known in spirituality circles and others never previously published, gave expression to a blessed way of living they had committed to. Those who were not clergy and religious were 'oblates', a state of life that necessitated some degree of commitment to living, adapted to their own particular circumstance, the monastic Rule of St Benedict of Nursia (c. AD 480–547) and some loose form of ongoing affinity with a specific Benedictine monastic community.

Intuitively I knew I had found something of value. With the summer approaching I committed to undertaking a programme of reading in Benedictine Spirituality. A Benedictine monk that I had met through my work came to mind, Fr Columba McCann OSB, of Glenstal Abbey, Murroe, Co. Limerick. I wrote to Columba and asked if he would be willing to review some notes that I would write. He kindly assented, opening a door to friendship as well as to spiritual and holistic guidance.

In the intervening years I have become a Benedictine Oblate affiliated to Columba's community, Glenstal Abbey. This in turn has come to influence many facets of my work. Through this book I am seeking to share some of the wisdom I have accrued with those who know or will soon come to know the joys, struggles, pleasures and challenges of serving on a Parish Pastoral Council. This is a constituency for which I have huge admiration: committed laity, clergy and religious committed to co-responsibility and willing to exert the service of leadership for the good of all. It is also a constituency for which I find myself praying increasingly. Why? Because I believe that among their ranks are many of the champions of tomorrow's Church and that parishes will find it difficult to survive without them.

Could the sixth-century Rule of St Benedict and contemporary expressions of Benedictine Spirituality have a contribution to offer Parish Pastoral Council members at this time? Over the coming chapters I propose to illuminate how they might help us in the absence of a more developed or accessible Parish Pastoral Council spirituality. This book will not speak about matters such as the importance of well-run meetings, hugely significant as such considerations are. Rather I believe our greater need is to get into our own heads and hearts, and to consider how we now see ourselves vis-à-vis participating in the mission of the Church. May you and others find something in these pages that will enrich your perception, experience and fruitfulness. The Lord desires our happiness and this must colour all that we do and commit to undertake, our thinking and our actions. The invigoration of Parish Pastoral Councils depends not just on the Holy Spirit but also upon our openness to his inspiration. When Eucharistic Prayer No. 1 is used during Holy Mass the words 'graciously accept this oblation of our service' encompasses the working of every Parish Pastoral Council in the world. The Christian life involves a degree of giving that exceeds the offering of our individual offerings to God. There is a very significant community dimension. The 'oblation of *our* service' assumes an openness to genuine partnership, to co-responsibility and most importantly, an ear attuned to our Creator Lord and to His creation.

People who exercise the service of leadership in Church contexts are by nature and Church design, a diverse and ever-changing lot characterised by a wide variety of charisms and frailties. Oblation, as illuminated via the Rule of St Benedict, has room for them all, as it is ultimately underpinned by a holy impulse not of our creation. For now, I invite you to hold to two commendations, encapsulated in the opening quotations of this introduction. I invite you to see yourself as being among the Lord's workers and to believe in your heart that your yearning for fullness of life is integrally linked to every invitation he sends your way to be in his service. I invite you to trust that his faithful love and constancy will support you in your struggle to be faithful, especially when his will is unclear to you, and to be open to the possibility that Pastoral Council activity can be a pathway for you and others toward greater closeness to God and neighbour.

In my opening recollection Francis, the man who rang me, was uneasy about serving as secretary of his parish's Pastoral Council. Unknown to himself he revealed a range of admirable capacities in that phone conversation: his capacity to review, to discuss, to foster relationship, to be a team player, to seek and take advice, to listen to others' concerns and to name and be proactive regarding his own concerns. His intuition that the new council could be impoverished if trust wasn't established was a correct one. Where clergy and laity fail to foster co-responsibility you may have a Parish Pastoral Council in name but never in reality.

In the end Maura and Francis decided to accept their fellow members' nominations and joined Fr Marcus as council officers. Trust did emerge and when the group met at the end of their term to review their experience all were appreciative of successes in the meantime. Their experience was also consistent with that of other councils known to me. In my experience, when faith-filled officers and members share a genuine concern for the well-being of their fellow parishioners, and when they find the courage to build on their abiding faith, good things evolve. Satan does throw an occasional spanner in the works but he tends to be unsuccessful when council members trust each other, are consultative, take time to pray and don't allow their unrealistic fears prevent them from giving new pastoral initiates a try.

We are, however, at something of a loss. By 'we' I mean those of us who serve on Parish Pastoral Councils and those of us who seek to support you.

Our bishops and others are to be commended for furnishing us, often after much consultation, with National Guidelines,[9] Diocesan Parish Pastoral Constitutions and Training initiatives. These are a great advancement on the provisions permitted under Canon Law in 1983. But do we need and are we ready for something more? It has taken time for me to realise and articulate it, but I think we, and those likely to serve with us, are now open to exploring our experience and of reaching for something more, something meaningful and authentic, something that will both support and challenge us to be the best we can be.

Through the remaining chapters I hope to speak to this space via a suite of insights and considerations grounded in Benedictine Spirituality and more specifically Benedictine Oblature. My desire is prompted by the moderate nature of this spirituality, its saturation in the word of God, its profound recognition of our human condition and the fact that it has helped me to become a happier and more trusting person. We all desire to be the best we can be. Whether you serve or have served on a Parish Pastoral Council for a term or a series of terms, this is Christ's desire for you too.[10] Time and again I will return to teachings encapsulated in the Rule of St Benedict that seek to support all of us. May the Lord support you in accessing and applying them to your life.

Notes

1   Pope John Paul II, Apostolic Constitution *Sacrae Disciplinae Leges* for the Promulgation of the New Code of Canon Law in *The Code of Canon Law in English Translation prepared by The Canon Law Society of Great Britain and Ireland in association with The Canon Law Society of Australia and New Zealand and The Canadian Canon Law Society*, London: Collins, 1983, p. xiii.

2   Pope John Paul XXIII, *Ad Petri Cathedram*, 61. For an excellent introductory article to the Second Vatican Ecumenical Council see Austin Flannery OP, 'Vatican Council II' in *The Modern Catholic Encyclopedia*, Collegeville and Dublin, 1994, pp. 888–895.

3   Canon 460.

4   Canon 511.

5   Canon 512, no. 1.

6   Canon 526, no. 1.

7   cf. 1 Jn 4:18.

8   Gervase Holdaway OSB (ed.), *The Oblate Life*, Norwich: Canterbury Press, 2008.

9   See Irish Catholic Bishops' Conference, *Living Communion: Vision and Practice for Pari Pastoral Councils in Ireland Today*, Dublin: Veritas, 2011.

10 cf. Jn 10:10.

Chapter Two

Discerning What We are About and God's Place in It

So I say to you: ask, and it will be given to you; search, and you will find; knock and the door will be opened to you.

(Lk 11:9)

First of all, every time you begin a good work, you must pray to him most earnestly to bring it to perfection.

(RB, Prologue, 4)

I have suggested that a rule of monastic life written by a sixth-century monk, St Benedict of Nursia, and a spirituality that derives from him and this Rule, has something precious to offer clergy, religious and laity who serve on Parish Pastoral Councils.

One hundred and thirty kilometres south-east of Rome rests the rocky hill of Montecassino. Here, in AD 529 Benedict established the monastery that he is most associated with, and it is here that he wrote his famous Rule. Over the centuries this monastery has been sacked, abandoned and rebuilt on numerous occasions. In 1944 it was completely destroyed by Allied bombing but today, thanks to the persevering efforts of many Benedictine monks and the assistance of the Italian government, a beautiful monastery bejewels the rocky rural landscape. Locally it is a towering symbol of resurgence. Older adults, who recall their parents and others speaking of war years recognise it as a testament to current peace. For the monks who live within its walls, it is a home characterised by a rhythm of prayer and work, time with visitors, one another and time alone with God.

Famous as this monastery is, it pales into insignificance when compared with the fame of St Benedict. He was born, a twin, to noble parents in AD 480 and died sixty-three years later in Montecassino in AD 543. For centuries he has been venerated in the Catholic Church, the Eastern Orthodox Church, the Oriental Orthodox Churches, the Anglican Communion and Old Catholic Churches – for example, those of the Union of Utrecht – and remains recognised by all as Europe's principal patronal saint. In his lifetime he founded twelve communities for monks at Subiaco, Lazio, Italy, about 65 kilometres to the east of Rome, before moving to Montecassino. His twin sister, Scolastica, was also attracted to monastic life, and founded a convent for women. Before their deaths he imparted his Rule to his brother monks, and today it remains available relatively unchanged. Since that time it has inspired and guided Benedictine, Cistercian and Trappist monastic communities and has long been recognised as St Benedict's greatest achievement.

St Benedict was not the first Christian monk to grace Italian soil. Scholars think it highly likely that he drew on an existing monastic document, 'The Rule of the Master', in crafting his Rule. They deem it highly probable that he adapted and edited this rule in light of his own considerable experience. Unlike other monastic rules, before and after, Benedict's Rule is humane, moderate and short. He was a man capable of and willing to draw on human experience, his experience and the experience of others. More significantly he neither expected himself or others to be heroes, recognising the importance of moderation and compassion. As one of his most famous biographers, Pope Gregory, noted Benedict 'wrote a Rule for monks that is remarkable for its discretion and clarity of language. Anyone who wishes to know about his life and character can discover exactly what he was like as an Abbot from his Rule, for his life cannot have differed from his teaching.'[1]

At the time of his death a great Gothic War raged all around Montecassino between the Byzantine Emperor Justinian I and the Ostrogothic Kingdom of Italy. It brought famine and devastation to the region and yet history records that Benedict's monks were to be found ministering to local communities, feeding them from their own reserves and intervening to prevent cruelty. Benedict is reputed to have died with his weakened arms lifted to heaven by his brother monks. Pope Gregory records that two of them had the same vision at the time, that of 'a magnificent road covered with rich carpeting and glittering with a thousand lights that reached up to heaven'.[2] In the course of the vision they were asked, 'Do you know who passed this way?' 'No,' they answered. A voice responded, 'This is the road which has been taken by blessed Benedict, the Lord's beloved, when he went to heaven.'

Though the appeal of monastic life, including Benedictine monastic life, has waned considerably in the postmodern Western world, thankfully there are still many Benedictine monasteries that live by the Rule of St Benedict. In many cases these Benedictine communities extend beyond their walls through their 'oblates'. What is a Benedictine Oblate? It is a woman or a man, who through association with a specific Benedictine monastery or convent, and adherence to the Rule of Benedict moderated to their personal circumstance, places his or her life at the service of God while remaining at home in the world, fulfilling their familial, work and other obligations. Today Benedictine Oblates are to be found associated with Benedictine monastic and convent communities on all continents and in at least thirty-six countries. Numbers are estimated to exceed twenty-five thousand.[3] The fact that monks would hold to a monastic rule for more than one and a half millennia is quite extraordinary. The fact that twenty-first century lay women and men, married and single, and secular clergy of different Christian denominations would apply such an ancient rule to their day-to-day living is something of an ever greater mystery ... or perhaps not.

Many of us experience a desire to place ourselves at the service of God while remaining in our own homes, communities or places of work. Fulfilling family and work obligations is something we do as a matter of conviction, habit and course. Though we may never get round to putting words on it, or formally think about it, we position ourselves in situations and social groups that we hold to be good for ourselves and others, situations we believe God wishes us to populate. Oblates are no different save that they are following a calling, or perhaps it would be better described as a personal intuition, to take an additional step. They 'attach' themselves, albeit loosely, to a particular monastic community devoted first and foremost to the praise of God. The reasons they do so are probably as numerous as themselves but somewhere in there is the desire to grow in a Benedictine Spirituality, supported by the prayer and witness of 'their' monastic community, including fellow oblates. They perceive a value, a pathway, to greater fulfilment and joy in committing to living the Gospel as proposed in the Rule.

This is very much a contemporary expression of oblature, a reflection of developments since the Second Vatican Ecumenical Council in the 1960s. Go back in time and one encounters a rather different but nevertheless significant understanding. Historians such as Judith Sutera recount that the word 'oblate' originally referred to a child offered by parents for religious life but that the expression soon grew to include children educated by monastic tutors before taking positions of influence and adult responsibility; for example, Charlemagne, Louis the Pious and Duke Henry II of Bavaria, Holy Roman Emperor, now honoured as a special patron saint of Benedictine Oblates. Sutera also records that as early as the mid-eleventh century, William, Abbot of Hirschau in Bavaria, Germany, established rules for two types of oblates, those living in monasteries without vows and those living 'in the world' but affiliated with a monastery.[4] In the eleventh century Pope Urban II (c. AD 1098) praised the latter practice as being in keeping with the spirit of the ideal Christian community proposed to us in the Acts of the Apostles.[5] Such oblates lived as lay persons but under obedience to their abbot.[6]

By the late Middle Ages, many pious lay people associated themselves with religious orders in one way or another – for example, lay associations and 'tertiaries' (third orders) – but Benedictine Oblates of the era held a unique space in so far as they committed through their rite of oblation to both the Benedictine Spirituality and a particular Benedictine monastic community. This continues to the present day.

In the 1940s G.A. Simon, a priest oblate of St Wandrille's Abbey in Normandy, France, also explored the history of Benedictine Oblature. He discovered that the monastic decadence of the fifteenth and sixteenth centuries necessarily involved decadence in oblature, but that the latter was not forgotten. It was at this time that the custom emerged, still voluntarily followed by some oblates, of wearing some mark or symbol of the order; for example, St Benedict medal or crucifix. He also notes that the seventeenth century saw some great oblate women, the most celebrated of whom was Helena Lucretia Cornaro-Piscopia of Padua (1646–1684). Helena, a prodigy of learning, piety and mortification, secretly consecrated herself to the Lord at the age of eleven. In 1669, at the age of twenty, she translated from Spanish into Italian *Colloquio di Cristo nostro Redentore all'anima devota* (*Dialogue between Christ Our Redeemer and a Devoted Soul*), a book by the Carthusian monk Giovanni Laspergio. As the fame of her intellectual accomplishment spread she was invited to join several scholarly societies and in 1670 became president of the Venetian society Accademia dei Pacifici (Academy of the Peaceful). Helena was also the first woman to receive a degree from a university, a doctorate in philosophy. Such was the intense interest in her studies that her defence was held in the Cathedral of Padua rather than the university.[7]

Simon also records that Benedictine Oblature followed the same destiny of the Benedictine Order in eighteenth-century Europe and shared in suffering its agony. It was revived in the nineteenth century by the first Abbot of St Peter's Abbey, Solesmes, France, Servant of God, Dom Prosper Guéranger. Once again oblates returned to the practice of visiting their monastery at least annually to renew their spiritual strength by praying with their monastic brothers or sisters and experiencing their hospitality. Biographies of a number of significant figures of the late nineteenth and early twentieth centuries also illustrate noted individuals about their ranks: philosophers Jacques and Raissa Maritain; distinguished English author, Rumer Godden; social activist and co-founder of the Catholic Workers Movement, Blessed Dorothy Day; and poet and essayist, Kathleen Norris.

Of course Benedictine Spirituality is but one of many enduring Christian spiritualities. Readers familiar with others, such as the Carmelite, Ignatian, Dominican and Franciscan spiritualities, will know that in each case, an individual person was central to their emergence. These persons – St Dominic, St Ignatius, St Francis – came to be recognised in their day above all else for their sanctity. Highly attuned to both the Spirit of God and human nature, they were persons who incarnated their desire for God and human happiness into values, attitudes and lifestyles that placed Christ and the mission of the Church at the epicentre of their worlds. And so it is not surprising that these spiritualities continue to look to their saint as well as to opportunities for direct encounter with Christ through scripture-based prayer and participation in the liturgy. Those who have committed to them as pathways to greater holiness seek in solitude and community to grow in love and service.

Now I anticipate some readers may be saying to themselves 'Well, that's all very interesting, but how does it relate to serving as a member or officer of a Parish Pastoral Council?' I propose to you one of two possibilities:

1. That among the ranks of 'oblates' in every century are persons who have found it necessary, in order to be true to themselves, to connect with a living spiritual tradition.
2. That God, knowing the struggles that face his disciples, has offered certain disciples the support of oblature and its corollaries that they might be further supported in fulfilling his will in their lives.

In living oblature there in an onus on the person to be attentive to God. By various means they look to God for inspiration, encouragement, hope, energy, deliverance and success. In an ideal world this would be common to all women and men of faith. For a Parish Pastoral Council to be successful, this needs to be characteristic of at least some of their time together. The oblate turns to the practices and tools of Benedictine Spirituality to assist them. Might the individual Pastoral Council member benefit from having their own toolkit? Or better still might the Pastoral Council benefit from periodically exploring its own need of spiritual and other nourishment?

In my experience we all need community and sometimes more than one. To belong to a family, a circle of friends, a club or association, a parish and the Church serves us well. Regarding each, there are those who serve, giving more of themselves, benefitting everyone. These people, in the parish context, ideally include the members of the Parish Pastoral Council.

During the tenure of our service it is important to note the voices we need to tend to and also our duty to be representative of various constituencies in our parish – young people, parents, those on the margins, all to whom Christ directs his gospel.

In this sense Christian living is often quite demanding. Increasingly it demands that we weigh up how we will utilise our time and abilities and discern, individually or collectively, how best to respond to the aspirations and needs brought to our attention.

In order to stay the course many Christians now find it necessary to work out how best to accept Christ's invitation 'to come away to a lonely place and rest a while' (Mk 6:31). For an oblate, it may be a visit to their monastery. But what about the Pastoral Council member who is no less pressed or in need of such sustenance? What about you and those who serve with you?

My learning, from being with Pastoral Council members who take time out from the hustle and bustle, is that they are the last to abdicate responsibilities or distance themselves from the emerging needs of their communities. Rather they tend to be people who take a less frequented approach to working out how they will honour, contribute and respond. They may never have seen the inside of a monastery or convent, but they have personal or collective mechanisms that incorporate creating space for prayer, spiritual input, opportunities for discussion, silence and, in some instances, participation in the Eucharist and Sacrament of Reconciliation. In short, they bring their lives and concerns, their engagements and related concerns to God. Molly, one such Pastoral Council member, also incorporates her favourite dessert, a big bowl of ice cream! In her case it's the few hours she spends a few times a year with her friend Magella at the National Shrine of Our Lady in Knock, Co. Mayo. 'This', she says, 'sustains me.' She also remarked recently that her participation in her parish's Pastoral Council meeting is always qualitatively different during a week after her afternoon in Knock. To quote her again, 'I am just more together!'

This recognition is highly significant and represents something wholesome and healthy. Some decades ago, oblature within certain monastic communities mirrored something spiritually, emotionally and psychologically unhealthy in some parishes. The self-emptying humility (explored in chapter seven) at the heart of oblation was eclipsed in deference to a benign form of servitude. Impacted oblates – many of their own choosing – expressed their oblature by being a volunteer in the monastery gift shop or farm. Their principal identification with Benedictine Spirituality was reduced to being a volunteer. There was nothing wrong with the gift of their time and work, but one more readily saw the problem when they presented attendance at one of 'Father's' spiritual conferences as a reward for their generosity.

Within parishes a genuine partnership between priests and laity is central to the well-being and proper functioning of every Parish Pastoral Council. There have been parishes, however, where lay involvement hasn't flowed from a spirit of co-responsibility as envisaged in baptism. Much to the disappointment of many clergy, the basis of serving can still amount to 'supporting Father' in his work. Where this has been characteristic of parish life over decades, it's quite difficult for a Pastoral Council or a parish as a faith community to thrive.

To this day many Catholics can feel quite inhibited in the presence of their priest. This is indicative of our need to evolve new ways of working with each other and perhaps there is some unlearning to be undertaken? I don't suggest this to judge or apportion blame or raise negative emotions.

From time to time I sit with priests and lay people from other countries and continents who have come to live and work among us. Though all are quite careful not to cause offence, they are very surprised at how underdeveloped our partnership appears to be. Though clergy are rarely native to the parish they serve in and can transfer to another parish, in Ireland we have been slow to shoulder the mantle of leadership with them. Some priests I know would also say privately that they were not trained to work with others – brother priests or laity.

In my experience persons nominated to serve on Parish Pastoral Councils are wholesome caring Christians with generous spirits who have much to offer. Only some councils, however, have evolved to embrace open discussion concerning their council's *raison d'être.* It can be easier to work to the premise that we know what we are about, lending a hand at the pivotal moments of the Church's year. It can be quite disconcerting when a prophetic voice from within the group invites us to consider whether everything is actually going well or whether something needs to be tended to, either for the sake of the parish or the proper functioning of the council?

The opening quotations of this chapter recall St Benedict's exhortation to begin every good work by praying most earnestly to God to bring it to perfection.[8] If the founding intention behind the establishment of a Pastoral Council is to be realised and flourish, then we do well to ask God to help us to bring it to perfection in our time. The quotation from Luke's Gospel reminds us of Christ's word to all of us: 'Ask, and it will be given to you; search, and you will find; knock and the door will be opened to you' (Lk 11:9). The key word here is 'ask' and to ask we must first name our need. Often we recognise a need but lack the courage to ask for help. Sadly, there is a grave danger when this is the case. We risk joining the Israelites in spending forty years wandering around the desert. Unmet challenges, no matter the cause, leave us where we are, rather than toward the Promised Land.

One of life's learnings for many oblates is that the spiritual life is ultimately a lifelong grace with which we do well to cooperate. On occasion this grace can lead to volatile moments. To feel, recognise, name and share certain tensions or frustrations in humble service to the truth takes an inner liberty. Every Parish Pastoral Council member is a Christian seeking to love God and their neighbour. We present because we care, but do we care sufficiently to risk being misrepresented as unappreciative, difficult or even 'a bit mad'? If all is truly well most of the time, our experience will tell us so. If it isn't, what is to happen? In my experience ignoring a problem, particularly a problem of a pastoral nature, culminates in further disappointment, frustration and distrust. Equally the price of beginning what we don't intend to complete can be high.

&. Martin was delighted to be nominated by his neighbours to serve on the Parish Pastoral Council. He had been away from the Church for a number of years but returned after the death of his father. What appealed to him was the care he and his family had encountered, not just on the part of the priest but also on the part of the Parish Funeral Team. The first meeting was very different from what he expected. He couldn't say why, but he thought it would be like school. Rather than the priest praying an Our Father or Hail Mary, they read the Sunday Gospel and talked about it. That part felt weird but good. It aroused his curiosity. Then the other members informed the priest who was sick in their areas and he confirmed that he had been in contact. Most of the remainder of the meeting focussed on prayer services for the dead during November. That was ok … but he felt he had nothing to offer, not being a person to read in public. Then the secretary read a letter from someone working for the diocese looking for views on a document, but no one expressed much interest.

The second and third meetings were very similar but on these occasions the focus was on Christmas and Lent. It was evident that Fr Mick appreciated some team support at these times. The meetings also tended to end in similar fashion, with Fr Mick and the chairperson thanking everyone for participating. Martin was conscious that he had never contributed.

He skipped the fourth meeting as he felt there was no point in going. When he missed the fifth he received a call from Jane, a neighbour and friend of many years. When he told her he didn't feel cut out for council meetings, her answer flabbergasted him: 'Sure that's the way most of us feel! Don't let that put you off.' He wasn't deterred. 'But Jane,' he responded,

'I know what it's like to be outside the Church, I thought we would be talking about how to help people to get back in!' 'I don't think there would be an appetite for that,' said Jane. 'We are not in the business of telling people how to live their lives anymore.'

Were Martin living in a dynamic urban parish in another country where Pastoral Council members receive training regarding a suite of parish ministries, I firmly believe he would have been commissioned as part of the parish's Baptism Team. The reality was that he was wonderful with ordinary people like himself. Bearing no airs and graces, they felt very at home with him. He communicated the wholesomeness of faith in a warm handshake, in standing with people, in offering a word of encouragement … and much as he valued parish liturgies at pivotal times of year, he wasn't built for that. Within three months he formally resigned from the Pastoral Council for 'personal reasons' but admitted privately to friends that he couldn't see a way of raising his concerns without offending the parish priest and chairperson and those members who genuinely believed (and were) making a valuable contribution. ❧

When inaction is underpinned by fear of fallout or something else we miss out on the life we were meant to have. It can also mean that we never come into the new and deeper levels of relationship with God and others that new directions herald. Those of us, like Martin, who experience a disconnect between our experience and inner desire, particularly in relation to something we believed would increase our sense of belonging and purpose, can feel a great loss. Another significant danger named by Benedict may also apply, i.e. the risk of losing the power of God that is within us. He states: 'With his good gifts that are within us, we must obey him at all times that he may never become the angry father who disinherits his sons and daughters … for refusing to follow him to glory.'[9]

Surely this quotation of Benedict's is not to be taken literally? Sr Joan Chittister, a renowned Benedictine spiritual writer, suggests such words were not idle metaphors in sixth-century Nursia and Montecassino. To be a member of a Roman family during St Benedict's lifetime was to live under the religious, financial and disciplinary power of one's father until his or one's own death. To lose relationship with him was to risk a greatly diminished life. Benedict's exhortation is thus not to disinherit ourselves by accepting a way of being that is unbecoming our dignity as children of the living God. 'With his good gifts that are within us' we are better equipped than we realise to honour him and to serve our neighbour in true humility and sincerity of heart. Utilising gifts such as courage, wisdom, understanding and piety, can also preserve us from the kinds of decadence that easily rob a Pastoral Council of its true spirit.

Over recent decades a significant percentage of Catholic parishes have been haemorrhaging young people, including young parents. It's uncertain as to how many will survive in their current state. There is a growing awareness that to survive and thrive many parishes will need to reorient to being 'intentional Christian communities' characterised by participatory opportunities that support belonging, evangelisation, catechesis and mission. Church will no longer be something we are born into but something consciously chosen by or for us. The transition from where we are to where the Lord wills to take us will not happen against our will. In that respect the choice is ours. God always respects our freedom.

In my diocesan work I already see signs of this great transition. It is evident in the attentiveness of an ever-increasing number of Pastoral Councils to the critical pastoral issues of our day – right relationship with God, belonging, good relations, the well-being of all, evangelisation, catechesis, stewardship and social justice. Contemporary faith will continue to be expressed sacramentally but, in keeping with the Gospel and the witness of our saints, will not be reduced to observance of religious prescriptions to which parishioners must ascend. Increasingly, I am seeing members of Parish Pastoral Councils rise to the challenge. The leadership they are exerting within their councils (they are not always officers) and parishes differs from the kinds we associate with charismatic political leaders, sporting heroes or savvy media magnates. Rather it's often borne of a simple faith and humble disposition, that whilst being respectful of everyone, recognises that life is too short to pass up opportunities for greater happiness. These are the women and men who see opportunities to forge new partnerships and to build bridges. What's beyond their sphere of influence they will leave to God. What's within it, they will honour; for example, a local environmental initiative in response to Pope Francis' 2015 encyclical *Laudato Si'* (On Care for Our Common Home).

But how are these good people, these builders of contemporary parishes, to be sustained and nourished, especially those who have yet to experience God through the sacraments or who have never experienced God's presence through *Lectio Divina* or other forms of scripture-based prayer?

How might they, like Benedictine Oblates, Third Order Franciscans, be imbibed by a great and living spiritual tradition? No one expects a manual labourer who has gone without food to be as productive as the one who has recently eaten. Equally, there is the matter of preference. When adults gather for a meal in a restaurant they like to choose for themselves. Through this book I am declaring my personal leanings toward Benedictine Spirituality as a source of inspiration and strength, and as a font of pure goodness. Others will propose that you draw from the wells of Franciscan, Jesuit, Dominican and other spiritualities. These too trace their roots back to holy men and women (don't forget Ss Scolastica and Claire) who modelled their lives on Christ and who, like him, were focussed primarily on God. Devoid of any form of teflon, they discovered in the evangelical counsels, chastity, poverty and obedience, the antidote to all forms of materialistic craving. Many of those who thread their way today also live simply and through education, communal supports and review opportunities are strengthened to counter the subtle influences that would have them be lesser Christians. They are our brothers and sisters in Christ and in my experience, very eager and willing to stand with us.

Benedict's Rule, however, stands out for me. It is quite remarkable in the manner it invites us to care about everyday things and relationships, or to put this another way, to witness to conservation. For the Benedictine monk, nun and oblate, even our kitchen utensils merit respect ... 'as if they were the sacred vessels of the altar'.[10] Return with me momentarily to the Parish Pastoral Council meeting that never encounters a perception such as this. My related questions are:

1. Might individual council members or councils as a whole be supported in their maturation and mission effectiveness by connecting in some way with this or another living spiritual tradition?

2. Does the absence of such a connection, go some way to explaining why some clergy and laity who serve on Parish Pastoral Councils are reticent about incarnating and embracing the Parish Pastoral Council ideal?

As Christians, we both need and value encouragement and direction. Frequently we look beyond ourselves though our faith encourages us to also look within. Many of us also find ourselves living alongside adults who are finding our contemporary materialistic secular way of life deeply unsatisfactory. Can they see in us a viable alternative? In recent years I have been conscious of the return of a significant cohort of adults to our churches for a time, but only some stay. Among them are those who have already taken a step toward a more evangelical way of living. In some instances they have recoiled from the hollowness of a life without God. For others, it strikes me as a beautiful grace received, a natural progression in genuine holiness. In both scenarios the Holy Spirit is at work.

In the days leading up to Pentecost the Roman Lectionary draws on Jesus' great prayer to God the Father (Jn 17) and the struggles of St Paul against the imperfect orthodoxy of his time (Acts 20–22, 28). Central to Jesus' prayer (Jn 17:1–3) is his desire to give us eternal life, which he defines as 'to know you, the only true God and Jesus Christ whom you have sent'. He also speaks of having passed God the Father's word to his disciples (Jn 17:14) and explains our alienation from the world as a significant consequence. According to Jesus, those who receive him as Lord and Saviour belong to the world no more than he does. Moreover they (we) require protection from the evil one (Jn 17:15), another Benedictine theme common to other Christian spiritualities. And so Jesus prays the Father will consecrate his disciples in the truth (Jn 17:17). To put this another way, Jesus desires that they (that is us today!) be set aside for dedication to God. He prays also for those who, through his disciples' teaching, will come to believe in him (Jn 17:20) that we may all be one (Jn 17:21) and that we may share in the divine life of the Blessed Trinity (Jn 17:21), that the love with which the Father loved Jesus may be in us and so that he (Jesus) may be in us.

God's choice of us is ultimately a choice to make us partakers in the divine life of the Blessed Trinity. It is here, in this awareness and realisation, that the interior joy of oblation proposed in Benedictine Spirituality resonates most strongly with many oblates. Something equivalent is known to clergy, religious and laity who live a Eucharistic spirituality, giving generously of themselves with heartfelt joy because of their awareness of all they have received. If God, who withholds nothing from us, and who has inspired countless saints, including Our Lady and St Benedict, to make a living oblation of themselves, might this also be his invitation to everyone open to serving on a Parish Pastoral Council? It is an important question, not in terms of active involvement in approved projects and initiatives but in terms of prioritising time with God and in allowing his influence to increasingly permeate our being and way of being in this world.[11] Of course, with regard to such matters, what stands to many oblates is their connection with a living praying community (monastery or convent). In reality this is but one of many paths open to those who wish to grow in holiness.

Let's imagine for a moment two Parish Pastoral Councils. The first comprises a group of very generous, highly competent, caring women and men who know one another from participating in Mass together on Sundays and who cross paths in the shops in their neighbourhoods. They meet monthly, tend to everything on their agenda and are valued for their contributions to parish life. Now let's imagine another council with a similar profile but in this instance a number of group members are also committed members of apostolic, missionary, scripture-based prayer groups and are inclined to devote a day or two in the year to their ongoing faith development. They too meet monthly and are valued for their contribution to parish life. Which in your view has the greater capacity to be of service to the Lord?

One of the most striking consequences of a meaningful engagement with any of the enduring Christian spiritual traditions is that it constantly elevates this and similar questions. The great teachers of these traditions constantly encourage their students to return to the scriptures and the sacraments as meeting points with Christ. For Benedictine Oblates the Rule of St Benedict offers a lens through which to see and ponder the Gospel, and much more importantly the Jesus behind it. It is very early days for Parish

Pastoral Councils but can they, or the faith communities they serve, really flourish without immersing themselves in Christ?

In introducing his Rule[12] Benedict represents the Lord standing in the market place calling out to the passer-by: 'Is there anyone here who yearns for life and desires to see good days?'[13] Benedict offers a salutary response, applicable to those moments when we, as baptised Christians, are invited to come into the service of the Lord. The way, initially, we are told, will be hard and narrow. There is no promise of light relief or shielding from the struggles rooted in one's own or others' inertia or spiritual decadence. All who wish to mature in faith are called to be open to sharing in the sufferings of Christ. That, however, is not the complete picture. He also promises that we, through patience (a gift of the Holy Spirit frequently brought to maturity through trials), will evolve hearts 'overflowing with the inexpressible delights of love' until at last we reach our heavenly home.

What's clear from the outset is that courage, another gift of the Holy Spirit, is also required. To say yes to undertaking a pastoral ministry or to serving on one's Parish Pastoral Council is to say yes to risk. The Parish Pastoral Council ideal, characterised by co-responsibility, partnership between priest and lay member, and a willingness to further the mission of Christ, is commendable and inspiring but it can also be perplexing. Minimise the risk for yourself and you may well minimise the outcome. The fact you are reading this book suggests you have embraced or may be about to embrace the risk. Lives lived in self-surrender to God still grapple with the challenges of discipleship. Might you draw on certain elements of Benedictine Oblature or some other Christian spirituality or practice as you make your way? Might you pray that God will direct you to what will suit you best and for the grace to see it when he responds?

Whatever you decide, know that God is with you.

Notes

1   *The Dialogues of Pope St Gregory the Great,* Book II, 36, available online at: http://a chive.osb.org/gen/greg/

2   Ibid., 37.

3   Judith Valente, 'Benedictine Oblates stand at a crossroads in monastic history,' published online by Global Sisters Report – A project of *National Catholic Reporter*, 27 November 2017: https://www.globalsistersreport.org/blog/gsr-today/trends/benedictine-oblates-stand-crosroads-monastic-history-50531

4   Judith Sutera, 'The Origins and History of the Oblate Movement' in Holdaway, *The Oblate Life,* pp. 31–38.

5   cf. Acts 2:42.

6   Ibid., p. 33.

7   G.A. Simon, *Commentary for Benedictine Oblates on the Rule of St Benedict,* ID: Mediatrix Press, 2016 (originally published in 1950 by St John's Abbey Press). See also: https://www.britannica.com/biography/Elena-Cornaro

8   RB, Prologue, 4.

9   RB, Prologue, 6–8.

10 RB, 31, 10.

11 cf. Rm 12:1–2.

12 As we shall see in later chapters, this Rule echoes the Gospel. One of my favourite inclusions, and one I have always found personally challenging is, 'No one is to pursue what he judges better for himself, but instead, what she or he judges better for someone else' (RB 72, 7). As I have grown in familiarity with the Rule, through contemporary commentaries as much as direct engagement, I've come to appreciate that much of its spirituality also finds resonance in contemporary Church teaching, including the increased emphasis since Vatican II on the vocation of the lay faithful. It also recognises our need of solid spiritual nourishment if we are to attain our true human potential.

13 This is the quotation cited at the beginning of chapter one, i.e. RB, Prologue, 14–15 quoting Ps 33(34):13.

Chapter Three

Obsculta, o fili:[1] Listening with the Heart

Thus says the Lord: 'For, as the rain and the snow come down from the sky and do not return without having watered the earth, fertilising it and making it germinate to provide seed for the sower and food to eat, so it is with the word that goes forth from my mouth: it will not return to me unfulfilled … and having achieved what it was sent to do.'
(Is 55:10–11)

Listen carefully, my child, to the master's instructions, and attend to them with the ear of your heart. This is advice from a father who loves you; welcome it, and faithfully put it into practice.
(RB, Prologue, 1)

❧ Joan jokes that she joined the Parish Pastoral Council to lose weight … a new Baking Club were meeting the same night and she desperately needed an alternative! When the Baking Club folded she announced that she was remaining with the council on account of the tea and chocolate biscuits served at the end of each meeting! In reality Joan is recognised in her parish community as a cheerful down-to-earth mother of abiding faith, who seeks to be good to her family and her neighbours. Through her good humour she brings a welcome sprig of joy to every council meeting. The other members value her capacity to lighten the mood when discussions become sombre. Another member of the same council, Pádraig, is more serious by nature but equally valued and respected. He exercises a much-appreciated vigilance regarding the care of the grieving and also serves with the parish's Bethany Bereavement Ministry Team. Like council members the length and breadth of every diocese, Joan and Pádraig contribute to the character of their council. Their personalities, ways of engaging in meetings and views on various issues shape every discussion and most outcomes. They, their fellow members and the members of all Parish Pastoral Councils are also gifted people. All of us have been granted a special charism (gift) by the Holy Spirit (cf. 1 Cor 12, CCC #2003) for the building up and benefit of our communities. Parish Pastoral Councils, ideally, offer an outlet for the expression of these charisms. ❧

Through my work, I occasionally have the privilege of facilitating a Pastoral Council undertake its annual review. This is a particularly gratifying experience when priest and lay members have established a solid partnership and agree on the mission of their council. In my experience this partnership both precedes and finds expression in fruitful outcomes. Most times these councils have allowed the work of coming to clarity to dominate a few meetings. Where these meetings have gone well, sometimes supported by an outside facilitator, respect, trust and comradeship have frequently been fostered, auguring well for future communication and project management.

In his book *City of God* St Augustine includes the following statement: 'The peace of all things lies in the tranquillity of order; and order is the disposition of equal and unequal things in such a way as to give to each its proper place' (XIX13). This is a touchstone of statecraft in our Roman Catholic tradition but it also has many other applications. As many of us know the role of 'parish priest' is a very responsible position. When relations between priest and lay members remain tentative and fragile then 'the tranquillity of order' necessary to support subsequent developments is absent. One sees this played out when clergy are reticent, and sometimes justifiably so, about sharing their pastoral concerns with lay members. It is equally apparent when members withhold views on important pastoral concerns for fear of offending their priest. In my experience many of us have invisible antennae that measure sincerity and authenticity. To put this another way, though we filter what we hear and see in light of our enculturation, we still hold a torch for the truth and when we encounter it we either resist it or go the extra mile.

In chapter two I offered a brief introduction to Benedictine Oblature, drawing on various and moderated applications of the Rule of St Benedict to situations other than monastic life. I have introduced this, not for its own sake, but by way of illuminating how other committed Christians open to participating in the mission of the Church are framing their personal response. I also queried whether elements of Benedictine Oblature, as a contemporary expression of Christian Spirituality, have something to contribute to the well-being of Parish Pastoral Council members, especially in aiding councils become more purposeful vis-à-vis the mission of the Church in the parish. In other words, I have queried if this spirituality has a valuable contribution to offer those of us who exercise pastoral leadership roles and if it can support the ongoing maturation of Parish Pastoral Councils.

Today, a vast array of commentaries on the Rule of St Benedict are available – medieval and contemporary.[2] Those I am familiar with, i.e. those pertaining to oblature, tend to highlight a number of key points, not unique to Benedict or his spiritual children.

1. Like many other masters of the spiritual life, St Benedict identifies God's continuous call and our response as the primary movement of the spiritual life. We can miss this when we see ourselves as the instigators or ultimate project managers of pastoral initiatives.

2. He strongly emphasises the importance of developing one's capacity to listen, thereby placing oneself in a better position to hear the Lord's invitations and to yield to his transformative power.

3. He avoids and discourages excessive asceticism or elevated experiences, emphasising instead continuous dedication to the basic dispositions that support personal, interpersonal and community growth.

Now what has this to do with Joan, Pádraig and other good people who serve on their Parish Pastoral Council, building bridges with parish priests and ensuring the productivity of Pastoral Council meetings? It is important as it illuminates our need to be good listeners ... and not just with our ears! Body language, tone, the kinds of question people ask, the range of insights people bring to discussions and what is left unsaid reveal a lot about a group. My knowledge and experience of this spirituality, suggests that, at the very least, it offers us a pathway into evaluating our experience. In essence Benedictine Spirituality is a healing spirituality, committed to 'the tranquillity of order', restoring order where it has been lost, feeding hope where it has either died or seemingly never dwelt. It doesn't require that we sign up to a constitution or policy framework. It doesn't even require that one become an oblate or a member of any other 'spiritual' grouping that requires a profession of faith or allegiance. What's key here, ultimately, is how this and other spiritualities help us to be our true selves with other people and with God.

Benedictine Spirituality invites those who investigate and yield to it, first and foremost, to be calm before the Lord, to learn to be more trusting of God, to communicate more directly with him and to open oneself to the possibilities of sharing in his joy, even in the face of suffering. Like other Christian spiritual treasure troves Benedict's Rule contains many insights that bid to be incarnated in day-to-day living.[3] Equally the Rule does not place an onus on anyone to radically 'convert' overnight. Rather, it seeks to further our relationship with God and one another in such a way as to support us to internalise core Gospel values and dispositions. This is not about adding to our activities, schedules and pressures. It is about helping us to see ourselves as God sees us, so that the love in which we are held can permeate our whole existence. It's about being in love in the same way that a husband and wife in a healthy relationship are in love after twenty or more years of marriage, allowing that love influence us to do small things differently.

When women and men are learning to drive, their driving instructors are constantly encouraging them to learn good driving habits – checking mirrors, using the brakes appropriately, etc. An oblate is someone who checks in with a spiritual driving instructor long after they have past their test. The value of this practice often finds expression in little but significant things; for example, in tweaking their approach to writing emails or texts, of making and taking calls, of taking time to invoke God's blessing on some initiative or person, especially when the hurt of a past encounter prevails. Why do they bother? Is it to grow in virtue? In my limited experience that is not the motivation. Rather it is as if their souls, by virtue of a grace received, want more. Like the taproots of great trees, they have identified where moisture is to be found and have begun to stretch toward it. My personal experience has encapsulated one other dimension. It has helped me to refrain from pouring lots of energy into projects and initiatives that have yet to be properly discussed and co-owned. I'm also more attuned to the corrosive murmurings of my own soul[4] and better at asking God to help me manage the temptations that I fail to manage, through dependence on my own resourcefulness.

Listening, and particularly listening with the heart, takes time and energy. We benefit from engaging with people who consciously or unconsciously foster this skill. I am possibly more fortunate than most in so far as my work and voluntary Church activities integrate opportunities for pastoral reflection with priests, deacons, catechists (through my work), fellow Benedictine

Oblates, Knights of St Columbanus[5] and ACCORD[6] volunteers. Being present with and to people who share their experiences and subsequent learning is a very grounding experience. It has also taught me that we are at our best when we actively seek and honour the holy in the ordinary, especially in its unfolding in our own communities. It helps with processing good and bad things that have happened that still pervade the mind. It allows me (and others) to be more attuned to the present moment and to avoid the superficiality that sometimes flows from holding too exalted an ideal of myself or others.

In short, taking time to stand back supports the emergence of new depths of understanding and appreciation in all of us. These new depths can assist us to recognise how even very small actions, something as simple as presenting our parish with an Agreed Report of a Pastoral Council meeting, can be both sacramental and sanctifying. It begins to dawn on us, if not already realised, that the Kingdom of God is manifested in every contribution to the cognitive, aesthetic and moral quality of the groups we share life with, including family. It has caused me to both question and reject all forms of rigidity that draw a sharp distinction between the sacred and the profane,[7] and to appreciate more fully Jesus' desire to be in intimate relationship with each of us and our communities.[8] By the grace of the Holy Spirit Christianity, as a way of life rooted in relationship with Jesus, continues to be modelled by communities throughout the world. At times we can feel as fragile as the first Christian community in Jerusalem, the one that sought to be 'faithful to the teaching of the apostles, to the brotherhood, to the breaking of bread and to the prayers' (Acts 2:42). No doubt those who exercised leadership among them frequently spoke about the challenges they encountered, but Christ, true to his promise (Mt 18:20), was in their midst, just as he is with us. In this Jerusalem group we have the precursor of our Parish Pastoral Council. Just as they sought to encourage and support their community through their struggles, so too must the contemporary Parish Pastoral Council.[9]

In my experience, if we, laity and clergy in parish settings, are to engage in such servant leadership, we must first invest in ourselves and commit to supporting our council to come to trust through mutual care and due regard for everyone's integrity. When we model principles of hospitality, community and good cheer, as advocated in the scriptures[10] and the Rule,[11] we pave the way for others to find themselves and to contribute. Council adaptations can more readily follow, particularly when supported by simple but frequent acts of kindness and hospitality, such as a regular text update or reminder of a meeting. When this value framework is established, group identity can find new and Christ-like expression,[12] taking the membership beyond their personal preoccupations with increased zeal for the possible.

Today many baptised Catholics pursue their desire for a meaningful spiritual life outside Church circles. Their perception and experience of Church to date can be a factor in their decision to do so. If they have been with us but without supports – particularly during formative years – to grow spiritually, then their decision is most understandable. These teenagers and adults are honouring their true nature but their spirituality can be sorely underdeveloped, and particularly when they remain at the mercy of the voices of contemporary culture that would reduce them to being consumers, service recipients and social media dependents. Moreover there can be times when we find ourselves among them. Our restless hearts need constant support if they are to remain attuned to God and neighbour.

❧ Mickey's youth had been marred by poverty. Like others of his community it was necessary for him to work from the age of twelve or so. He worked hard for thirty-five years, until illness forced early retirement. Then, his wife Maura died and for a time he felt completely heartbroken. He found consolation in the Mass and got quite a shock when two of his friends asked him if they could nominate him to the Parish Pastoral Council. He didn't say it to them but his initial reaction was 'But that's for educated people'. Two years into his three-year term and he discovered that others on the council liked when he spoke and tended to agree with him. He had the knack of naming stuff in a way that everyone understood. Fr Pat, his PP, was also glad of Mickey's contributions. He could see that Mickey had thought about the items on the agenda in the light of his own and others' experiences. Invariably Mickey's suggestions, though few and far between because he felt inhibited, were supported. Another reason was because the council members knew Mickey would be the first to put his energy behind them. He only encouraged what he believed, like the time he proposed and organised a pre-summer meeting with parishioners who had children with autism. Without Mickey there would have been no summer camp for those children or their families that year. ❧

But what if this does not describe the tenor or flavour of your experience of Pastoral Council meetings? What if heart and minds on your council conspire to get meetings over and done with as expediently as possible? What if there never appear to be grounds for a meaningful discussion with others between meetings? What I am proposing, in light of St Benedict's insights, is that the solution may not be, indeed it is highly unlikely to come from a group review meeting. Rather it is far more likely to be the consequence of a single member's humility, soul searching and positivity. There are people like Mickey on every Pastoral Council in the world, wholesome empathic people who read their local community with the eyes of Christ and who, when supported, find ways of responding to felt needs.

The power of our individual personal spiritualities should never be underestimated. St Benedict was attuned to this and allowed it to influence how he wrote his Rule, especially the latter chapters. He does not present as a Spiritual Taskmaster demanding conformity. Rather, like other Spiritual Masters – St Ignatius of Loyola and St Dominic – he presents as one who loves us and who, if allowed, will accompany us toward fullness of life in Christ. He is sensitive to the fact that no one grows by simply doing what they are coerced to do. Real growth, particularly in the Spirit, is always preceded by a personal willingness to grow. Spirituality only flowers in those who come to a personal decision to develop and who have the scope and support, frequently through some Church involvement or charitable enterprise, to do so.

Over the centuries it is quite probable that people have had diverse reasons for seeking to become oblates. Equally I anticipate that many current oblates remain with this form of Benedictine Spirituality for reasons other than those that inspired their original commitment. Either way, the central axis of this spiritual pathway – to allow the love of Christ come before all else[13] as we hasten toward our heavenly home[14] – remains sacrosanct. Oblates hold this in common with millions of other Christians and thankfully we continue to be encouraged and supported by the good teaching and preaching of ordained ministers and catechists. Equally, by virtue of my work within the Elphin diocese in particular, I am conscious of the acute pastoral sensitivities some clergy and other pastoral workers meet with periodically. Pastoral Councils, in my experience, are greatly supported in discerning their mission when clergy, with due discretion, communicate the considerations that tax their sense of purpose and ministry. Equally clergy can be greatly supported in knowing the questions and concerns that prevail among the faithful, so these can inform their prayer, study, discernment and preaching. Such need has been particularly prevalent in Ireland around referenda concerning abortion, marriage and blasphemy. We must allow too for the unique and private concerns and challenges of all Pastoral Council members, clergy, religious and lay. For an individual to serve while simultaneously contending with a new infirmity or undisclosed illness is not unusual. It behoves us all to make allowances, though not to the point of leaving a parish like an unpiloted and unmoored boat in the middle of a lake on a stormy night. If our listening with the heart tells us something is amiss, we need to honour it, not just pray that it go away or not lead to undue stress for others.

Another challenge can be to allow each member's network of relationships within the local faith community and their senses of the pastoral priorities to colour engagement. This, for all its messiness, frequently empowers councils toward meaningful and valued action. During the early stages of the global Covid-19 pandemic many sporting, cultural and Church organisations undertook audits by way of establishing how they could support the most vulnerable members of their communities. I was very struck by the leadership exerted by Fr Tony. He 'inherited' a Pastoral Council of eight members with whom he enjoyed working. When the pandemic struck he realised there were regions of the parish without representation and so, with the help of the other members, new representatives were sought and were informed that they need have no concern other than the well-being of everyone in their area. Afterwards Fr Tony shared a lovely observation, i.e. that the divine call–human response movement of the spiritual life never confines itself to our structures or our faith community. In one region of the parish the person most frequently nominated by committed community members was not a Catholic! Thankfully there continue to be great women and men of faith beyond the fold, who, without fuss or fanfare or any desire for recognition, teach us what it is to be a person of faith.[15]

Earlier in this chapter I noted the unique character of every Parish Pastoral Council. While it is true that the character changes as the membership changes, it remains within the competency of every Pastoral Council to enliven everyone's faith and charitable practice. This brings me to another critical characteristic of Benedictine Spirituality, 'honouring the personal within the collective'. Did you notice the personal nature of the opening lines of the Rule of St Benedict, quoted at the beginning of this chapter?

> Listen carefully, my child, to the master's instructions, and attend to them with the ear of your heart. This is advice from a father who loves you; welcome it, and faithfully put it into practice.[16]

Benedict speaks as a loving father calling his children into relationship with our heavenly Father. Momentarily he stands in the place of Christ, our gateway to the Father (Jn 10:9). He gets straight to the point when he tells us, 'the labour of your obedience will bring you back to him from whom you have drifted through the sloth of disobedience.'[17] Scholars suggest he is drawing on Baruch here: 'As by your will you first strayed from God, so now turn back and search for him ten times harder; for as he has been bringing down those disasters on you, so will he rescue you and give you eternal joy' (Bar 4:28).

For Benedict, obedience is one of three fundamental dispositions every Christian does well to hone. The root of our English verb 'to obey' is derived from the Latin words *ob-audire*; *ob* being a prefix meaning 'to or toward' and *audire* meaning 'to listen or to hear' (think of audio). Thus the great exhortation here is that we turn the ear of our heart to the advice of a loving father, God our Father. Benedict's premise is very straightforward. Through an open-hearted, attentive and intelligent listening to God, his love can come to fruition in us. This is our doorway to holiness and our model, with regard to such listening, is not Benedict but Christ.

All Benedictine Spirituality writers that I have read concur that obedience is about especially good hearing, about listening very attentively. What they illuminate is a far cry from the images of servitude, domination, blind obedience and unreasonable despotism sometimes associated with obedience in contemporary culture. The Benedictine view is squarely localised in 'blessing'. To promise obedience is to commit wholeheartedly to one's personal growth in Christ and to loving Christ 'above all things'.[18] Behind Benedict's encouragement to us to learn 'to hear with the ear of the heart'[19] lies a prayer that we would grow in our openness to unanticipated possibilities as much as to those we anticipate.[20] It calls on us to remain personally open and attentive to the various appeals persons and situations present to us as well as what arises during times of prayer and participation in the sacramental and charitable life of our Church. The hope is that over time we become less phased or dismissive of challenges that are not to our taste or perspective, mindful that God may well be at work in the resistance we are encountering.

    ❧ For five years Fr Ben followed the practice of his predecessor in meeting each of the Pastoral Councils of the three church areas in St Columbanus' Parish six times a year. Attendance at meetings tended to be 50 per cent and never exceeded 60 per cent. On turning seventy he communicated to the three councils his diminishing energy and his desire the three councils would form one Parish Pastoral Council. Half the membership was fine with it. Half were opposed. I was invited to facilitate a joint meeting. Fr Ben communicated that he would respect the outcome. In the hour-long discussion that followed not a single pastoral need was raised. Emotions were high. Representatives of two church areas were indignant. To have lost their resident priest ten years ago was sufficient humiliation. To lose their council would be another. Consequently I enquired about what successes the council had enjoyed that might be jeopardised. None were mentioned. I reframed the question: 'How has the council been a support to the pastoral life of the church area these past three years?' Fr Ben, uncomfortable with the silence, spoke about a time five years earlier when the council had played a role in fundraising for a car park and members had accompanied him to meetings with local government officials. He also spoke about his visits to the schools.

A week later I rang Fr Ben to see how he was doing. Not a man to let the grass grow under his feet he told me he had rang everyone who came to the meeting to thank them and had reiterated to them that he was feeling his years. He noted their empathy and also the fact that more were sympathetic to his request. A large percentage had also communicated that they felt they were the wrong people to serve on the council but that they would be happy to assist him privately anytime. They also reiterated the desire within their communities to hold to their church area identity, some dating back to Patrician times. They could also now see that this didn't militate against having one Pastoral Council that would help him in his work. I thanked Fr Ben for sharing and kindly suggested he had missed the essence of my question … how was *he* a week on from the meeting? 'I'm doubtful Justin. These, as you have seen, are good and earnest people but I'm not sure that moving from three councils to one will alter the fundamental problem. They see this as my parish and if I'm honest that suits me too most of the time.' ❧

What I find most heartening and now know from personal experience, is that those who seek to be true to God and attentive to self are not left alone. When it comes to doing the right thing we can anticipate the continuous encouragement and assistance of the Holy Spirit. As the quotation from Isaiah at the beginning of this chapter reminds us, no word of God returns to him 'unfulfilled or before having carried out my good pleasure and having achieved what it was sent to do' (Is 55:11). This is a liberating text for true disciples, especially those eager to respect the legitimate authority of others, be they clergy, teachers, healthcare workers, craftsmen, managers or community representatives.

Here too it is good to recall that the world in which St Benedict crafted his Rule was in a mess. Defective leadership, community dysfunction, abuse of power and privilege, and failure to support timely interventions contributed greatly to human suffering. This state of being formed the backdrop to Benedict's aspiration to create monastic strongholds capable of withstanding such destructive forces. The fact they became potent symbols of benevolence in the wider community is a testament of his success. These 'worlds apart' that welcomed visitors as they would welcome Christ[21] had ways of listening to human experience and to God very uncharacteristic of the world at the time. In each instance the abbot was a key figure, by virtue of his core responsibilities.

More specifically Benedict charged each abbot 'to regulate and arrange all matters that souls may be saved and the brothers may go about their activities without justifiable grumbling'.[22] Living the Rule promoted a dynamic harmony without making excessive demands on anyone. It was achieved not merely by adherence to some objective standard but by constant personal fine-tuning on the part of community members. They became attuned to listening to their situation, to developing a pastoral sensitivity to the concrete reality of life among themselves in the light of the Gospel. While monks were obligated to obey their abbot, he was also required to consult them on all-important matters.[23] Furthermore, before concluding with an invocation of divine blessing Benedict encourages all members of each community to adopt a position of 'mutual obedience' with the profound words:

> 'They should each try to be the first to show respect to the other' (Rm 12:10), supporting with the greatest patience one

another's weaknesses of body or behaviour, and earnestly competing in obedience to one another. No monastics are to pursue what they judge better for themselves, but instead what they judge better for someone else. Among themselves they show the pure love of sisters and brothers; to God, reverent love; to their prioress or abbot, unfeigned and humble love. Let them prefer nothing whatever to Christ, and may Christ bring us all together to everlasting life.[24]

My story about Fr Ben has a happy ending. When he retired five years later the greatest blessing he gave his successor was the new Parish Pastoral Council. There was a new energy when the new council formed, each of the three church areas were represented by three parishioners. They had also nominated a parishioner known to them all, a past secretary of a club in the parish who was exceptional. The business of Church identity no longer resonated as before. One critical aspect was that two new members were young parents concerned about the transition of the faith to their children. Others were newcomers to the parish, eager to belong. One member worked with a counselling service and was very attuned to the importance of spirituality for silent sufferers in every community. Fr Ben gave thanks to God for giving him the courage to both facilitate and lead the change. His obedience to an inner intuition had worked out, not least because key values came into the light.

St Benedict's early life was typified by struggle, his own and the personal struggles of his monks. Analysis of his Rule suggests he frequently pondered both the meaning and example of Christ's suffering and the fact that Christ learned obedience to God the Father's will through suffering.[25] We also have St Paul's teaching that Christ 'when he had been perfected, he became for all who obey him the source of eternal salvation' (Heb 5:9). When we look to the lives of many Christian martyrs, we see that many have followed the path he trod, holding in faith to the resurrection on the last day. Their experiences and testimonies remind us that listening with the heart to God the Father does not always lead to 'human' successes and happy outcomes. Some, like Christ, have found themselves grappling with seemingly total failure, ignominy, suffering, abandonment and death. They too have been left with nothing but their reliance on God's trustworthiness. Sadly, we have Christian brothers and sisters in countries where the persecution of the faith means this could be their experience also. For them and others 'the labour of obedience'[26] of which Benedict writes is quite profound.

Currently, however, what can be much more pervasive and challenging regarding the harmony of a greater number of Parish Pastoral Councils are diverse, strongly held views regarding the celebration of the liturgy in the parish. Many of us, through the experience of family and work life, are accustomed to give and take, mutual forgiveness, the balancing of rights and on occasion, putting the interests of the family or another person before our own. This, indeed, is part of the unfolding of the paschal mystery in our lives. It is not surprising therefore that an increasing number of lay women and men are raising questions regarding those elements of the liturgy that are open to local contextualisation. On such occasions obedience can demand an informed, intelligent and patient search for the right way forward. The danger is in ignoring the need or demeaning the liturgy to being the preserve of a select few such that parishioners begin to go elsewhere. In such cases our obedience may require a simple acceptance of things, situations and persons that are less than ideal. At such times it can be good to ponder the insight of Benedictine nun, Maria Boulding OSB. In an address to oblates she noted that:

> Amid the concrete realities of the Church, in skirmishes on the parish front or frustration with the local liturgy, there is scope for patient, faith inspired obedience. Your most fundamental

obedience to God may be acceptance of yourself – yourself as you are, with all your particular strengths and weaknesses, your gifts and limitations, all the baggage you carry from your remote and immediate past, all that your life has made you. Such a person is what God wants, and you must want it too; but such obedience is not a static programme, because it means consenting to become through God's grace the person he wants you to become … To accept yourself and other people, to accept joyfully the conditions of life in a flawed, inconsistent, sinful but redeemed humanity, is an obedience to the creator.[27]

This type of obedience, in my view, requires a deep listening to self, God and others. According to St Paul 'if we (our faith community) live by the truth and in love, we shall grow completely into Christ' (Eph 4:15). It is good that the culture of our councils would be characterised by open and informed discussion but we must also be open to letting go desires, dreams and personal preferences, to unlearning and learning anew, to dying to self, sometimes in an extended way over the term of a council. This is where listening and ongoing conversion meet. A garden when tended, yields extraordinary graces and blessings, but when unattended spreads weeds beyond its borders.

Councils benefit greatly when individual members consider why they serve. For some it can be important to have an objective; for example, during my years of service I will seek a, b and c for our parish. A culture that supports good discussion generally serves everyone very well but it also necessitates an intelligent, patient and conscientious engagement, one that incorporates a local reading of the signs of the times. It can also require some reorientation on the part of some members, a naming of why a particular item is on the agenda, our sense of our council's role in discussing it and a commitment to decision-making by consensus (no point in members subsequently feeling aggrieved and seeking an opportunity to reverse the decision later).

There can also be times when serving requires a willingness on our part to be stretched, to go the extra mile.[28] This occasionally occurs when a council invites a reticent member to serve as chairperson or secretary. It does not mean that she or he should accede. Rather, obedience would suggest the person examine the basis of his or her reticence. Whole councils can also have the experience of being invited to stretch themselves. Recently Fr Luke requested that the entire Pastoral Council join him in undertaking an Alpha course. Members agreed, but not without reservation. During the weeks of the course they lost a number of members, but at the time of writing that council is among the more comfortable promoters of a new evangelisation.

Much more could be written about 'listening with the heart' but that will be for others to honour. We need to move on. I began this chapter with some of the most loved and reassuring lines of the Hebrew Bible (Old Testament):

> Thus says the Lord: 'For, as the rain and the snow come down from the sky and do not return without having watered the earth, fertilising it and making it germinate to provide seed for the sower and food to eat, so it is with the word that goes forth from my mouth: it will not return to me unfulfilled or before having carried out my good pleasure and having achieved what it was sent to do.' (Is 55:10–11)

I also drew attention to the opening line of the Rule of St Benedict:

> Listen carefully, my child, to the master's instructions, and attend to them with the ear of your heart. This is advice from a father who loves you; welcome it, and faithfully put it into practice.[29]

Almost fifteen hundred years ago a loving father figure, the abbot St Benedict, came to know through his own life experiences the truth of this scripture. He also opted, in keeping with the tradition of the time, to use the phrase 'Listen carefully, my child' to capture the essence of what he proposed through his Rule. Though he had a considerable wealth of experience to impart, he did not orient his reader to listen to him. Rather, through reference to 'the master's instructions', he invited his monks to listen primarily to God as they pondered his words.[30] Today, recognition of the value of his Rule extends far beyond Benedictine monasteries and convents. One reason for this is that it encapsulates many insights that are also present in sacred scripture, the writings of other saints and the lived experience of many Christians. The Rule, however, does give prominence to listening. Those of us raring children or who can recall the benevolent parenting we received will appreciate why this is so. We know first-hand its capacity to enhance every aspect of life. It is difficult to impart knowledge and skills to those who have difficulty listening, those ultimately too preoccupied or busy to learn.

To train oneself or another to listen attentively to the voice of God, the voice of conscience and the complementary voices that lead us to true fulfilment will forever be both challenging and worthwhile. The medium of a Parish Pastoral Council provides a particular space, for those who can recognise it.

In exploring this I have drawn on Benedictine Spirituality, particularly Benedictine Oblature. Grounded in the gospels, the sacramental life of the Church and the Rule, it suggests the development of a listening disposition as critical to progressing the mission of each council.

This spiritual pathway, though it prioritises attentive listening, does not propose that it alone suffices. It also advocates our continual growth *stabilitas* (incorporating balance and moderation) and *conversatio morum* (daily attentiveness to conversion of heart, permanently striving to improve one's attitude and participation in community life as an expression of one's desire for union with God). These, and how they may be applied, will be the focus of the next two chapters, helping us, I hope, to recognise how we can build our personal capacity to contribute, as well as our council's capacity to make a valuable contribution during the course of its term.

Notes

1   This is the Latin phrase with which St Benedict begins his Rule. It literally translates as 'Listen, O son'. At the time of writing, Benedict had his monks in mind. The broader application of his Rule only became apparent later.

2   See the select bibliography at the end of this book.

3   RB 4, 32, 40, 53:1.

4   For the dangers of such grumbling and murmuring, see RB 5:14–19.

5   For more on this Irish Fraternal Apostolic Association, see: www.knightsofstcolumbanus.ie

6   The Catholic Marriage Care Service of the Irish Catholic Bishops' Conference.

7   RB 31:10, 32.

8   cf. Jer 29:11; Mt 10:29–31; Eph 1:4–5; Jn 10:10; Jn 4:14; Rv 21:3–4.

9   Regarding matters of enduring challenge councils must be careful not to allow matters to fester or become exhaustive or oppressive. Even when experienced as a sharing in the sufferings of Christ (2 Cor 1:5; Lk 9:23; Phil 3:10) officers of Pastoral Councils, like individuals, are wise to seek support.

10   cf. Gn 18:1–10; Lk 14:13; 1 Pt 4:9; Rm 12:13; 1 Tm 3:2; Heb 13:13.

11   RB 42:10, 53:1–6.

12   cf. Jn 21:9–14.

13   RB 4:21.

14   RB 73:8.

15   cf. Mt 8:10–13.

16   RB, Prologue, 1.

17   RB, Prologue, 2.

18   RB 5:2, 72:11.

19   RB, Prologue, 1.

20   An excellent example is M. Basil Pennington OCSO, *Listen with Your Heart: Spiritual Living with the Rule of Saint Benedict,* Massachusetts: Paraclete Press, 2007.

21   RB 53:1–6.

22   RB 41:5.

23   RB 3.

24   RB 72.

25   cf. Heb 5:8; Phil 2:6–11.

26   RB, Prologue, 2.

27   Maria Boulding OSB, 'Obedience' in Holdaway, *The Oblate Life*, p. 174.

28   cf. Mt 5:40–41.

29   RB, Prologue, 1.

30   Basil Pennington, *Listen with Your Heart*, pp. 1–3.

Chapter Four

Stabilitas: Sticking with It and not Walking Away

Then Jesus said to the Twelve, 'What about you, do you want to go away too?' Simon Peter answered, 'Lord, to whom shall we go? You have the message of eternal life, and we believe; we have come to know that you are the Holy One of God.'

(Jn 6:67–69)

If he promises perseverance in his stability, then after two months have elapsed let this rule be read straight through to him, and let him be told: 'This is the law under which you are choosing to serve. If you can keep it, come in. If not, feel free to leave.'

(RB 58:9–10)

We have been exploring how elements of Benedictine Spirituality, as proposed in the Rule of St Benedict, can nurture and support adults who serve on Parish Pastoral Councils. More specifically we have drawn on some of the practices, undertakings and modes of thinking associated with Benedictine Oblature. We will continue in this vein in this chapter, principally by way of giving readers a mechanism to touch base with themselves.

Some Benedictines, like members of other spiritual families in the Church (Jesuits or Dominicans) like to draw on catchphrases that encapsulate what they hold dear. My favourite from the Rule of St Benedict is 'That God may be glorified in all things'.[1] 'All things' in this instance encompasses everything – relationships with family and friends, one's work, studies, one's prayer, church affiliation, recreation, even one's relationship with one's enemies, and in a special way, one's personal contribution to the mission of the Church. This catchphrase and similar ones – for example, 'Restore all things in Christ'[2] and the Jesuit Latin motto, *Ad maiorem Dei gloriam* (rendered as the abbreviation AMDG) meaning, 'For the greater glory of God' – can speak to our hearts in different ways at different times.

As a teenager I recall struggling with the Jesuit motto, doubting my capacity to be so pure in intention, to exercise such zeal. What I failed to realise was that those living these maxims were living them 'with God' as distinct from 'for God'. As my understanding grew, principally through the ministry of those who opened the scriptures to me, so too did my appreciation of the true adventure of faith. How different it is to say, 'That God may be glorified' when Matthew 10:29 – 'Can you not buy two sparrows for a penny? And yet not one falls to the ground with your Father knowing.'[3] – has taken root in one's heart. This and other comforting passages[4] remind us of how cherished we are. Nevertheless it takes a fair degree of trust, a capacity easily wounded, to take this reassurance to heart. The idea that God our Father charges himself with the defence of all Parish Pastoral Council members who seek to be true to the faith is not easily grasped. If our initial experience is less than positive we can also struggle to recognise council meetings as places where God is actually at work.

Last year Bishop Kevin Doran invited clergy and lay faithful to participate in a review of the Elphin diocese's Constitution for Parish Pastoral Councils.[5] This year, at Bishop Kevin's request, I established a diocesan group to: 1) assist parishes to establish new Pastoral Councils; 2) support the ongoing formation of existing Parish Pastoral Councils. As part of our work we met with clergy and laity to review training and other needs. Participants welcomed the opportunity to come into conversation and once again the commonality of needs across parishes was recognised.

During the course of our discussion St Peter's question to Jesus came to mind: 'Lord, to whom shall we go? You have the message of eternal life, and we believe; we have come to know that you are the Holy One of God' (Jn 6:68). Though different senses of the mission of the Church were articulated we were one in our acceptance of Jesus as Lord. What ultimately binds us, I realised, is our faith in him and our desire to return love for the love we know in him.

And yet, being human and keeping human company, many of us encounter a particular struggle when it comes to the incarnation of the parish and Parish Pastoral Council ideal. Individually and collectively we can find ourselves struggling perhaps more than God intends. From my experiences with councils I believe three things are important to avoid:

1. Throwing in the towel.
2. Members becoming entrenched around divergent visions or avoiding topics on which people may disagree.
3. Carrying on as if everything is fine when it's not.

The hazard of a brief list like this is that it can overshadow the wholesome goodwill, growing competencies and successes of many Parish Pastoral Councils. Since 2000 I have witnessed many Pastoral Council led initiatives. These have included parish and priest jubilee celebrations, events recognising the valued contributions of key parish personnel, fundraisers for pastoral initiatives, youth ministry and adult faith development initiatives and outreach initiatives in favour of elderly parishioners. In each instance individual members were hugely instrumental through every stage – planning, resourcing and overseeing – frequently encouraged and mentored by experienced clergy, parish secretaries and catechists. Today, thankfully, a growing number of clergy are strong advocates of increased lay involvement in such spheres of

Church life, eager for laity to meaningfully experience both the joy and struggle of sharing the gospel. Thankfully too, numbers of lay people are deriving joy from encountering and using the Spirit-given charisms gifted to them by God for the benefit of others in their community.

Such developments augur well for the future stability of parishes. We may, however, need to reflect more on how we express hospitality and belonging. This fundamental hallmark of Judaism and Christianity can occasionally be overlooked, with striking consequences.

    ❧ Two years ago, as I was leaving a national meeting in Dublin, a young GP serving a rural community asked to speak with me. He identified himself as 'a nominal Catholic' with the permission of a patient to seek advice from people who could be helpful. The patient was a non-Irish priest in his forties, Fr Max, who had acquired a dependence on a medication prescribed by this young doctor. The doctor had come to question his original diagnosis.

    Fr Max had arrived in Ireland following completion of some postgraduate studies in Rome. Having grown up in a parish greatly influenced by Irish missionaries he had been looking forward to his three-year term in Ireland. Sadly everything differed hugely from his expectations. In more than ten years of ministry it was his first time to be in a parish without a Pastoral Council, Catechist, Liturgy Group or to be serving two church communities where the only common denominator appeared to be himself. Apart from his availability to preside at Mass, sign Mass cards and look after funerals most lay people seemed indifferent to his presence. It was also his first experience of living in a presbytery where the phone rarely rang. He had never previously worked as a priest without weekly contact with other priests and had never been without some form of committee work that brought him into dialogue and ultimately friendship with parishioners.

He had shared with his doctor that it was customary in other countries for parishioners to introduce their priest to their families, friends and other networks but that wasn't his experience in Ireland. The doctor also shared that Fr Max had come to him on the advice of his spiritual director, who had advised him to get to know his daily Mass congregation. Fr Max had tried to do this, he said, but had felt they were suspicious of him, a view that influenced the doctor's decision to prescribe medication. Later, however, the doctor, based on his own discreet research, found cause to question 'the strange dynamic in that parish'. The parish had communicated to the bishop that they wanted a resident priest but now that they had one again, didn't appear to have any desire to engage with him!

Though the situation pertained to a diocese in another province I departed our conversation sharing the doctor's concern. A few phone calls and a week later Fr Max had two visitors. Maura and Tommy introduced themselves as newcomers to the parish too, having arrived about six months before Max. They invited him to accompany them to the parish GAA social on Friday night and Maura would countenance no refusal! There they and others, seamlessly orchestrated by an officer in the club that a priest friend of a friend had contacted, made a point of ensuring Max felt very welcome.

Max was also taken by surprise when the club's chairwoman announced his presence and he received a resounding round of applause 'for coming to them'. It was clear to all that the appreciation was for his presence in the GAA club, the social hub of the parish, a place where everyone was welcome. As the function progressed many people made a point of saying hello to Max. Some shared that owing to their personal circumstances – for example, divorce or sexual orientation – they no longer attended Mass but they still saw themselves as Catholic, wished him well and would be happy to be of assistance if he ever needed any help. Others asked for prayers owing to special needs. Others, he recognised from Sunday Mass, and was glad to get to speak with them. In short, it was the beginning Fr Max had anticipated when he took up his appointment … and within four weeks he was off all medication. The other great winner, to my mind, was the local doctor. I will forever remember his parting comment: 'It's amazing what a community can do when they know there's a problem! You know there are dimensions to the Catholic Faith I never considered!'

By an extraordinary turn of events I was also to learn more about the impact of this event on Maura and Tommy. At the time of the GAA social they were about fourteen months in the parish, having relocated after retiring from professional roles in Dublin. They too were quite taken aback by the experience of relocating but unlike Max, were at least in a position to process it together. The one place they felt they would be welcomed was Mass, but for the first three Sundays, though people smiled and nodded, no one spoke to them! They decided to visit one or two other churches in the area, only to have the same experience. When their adult children and grandchildren came at Christmas they opted to bring them to the 1 p.m. Mass in the local town because 'at least the children would see other children there, and that priest always made a point of welcoming the stranger'.

They kept their thoughts to themselves and it was only when they were asked if they could help Fr Max feel at home in the community that they realised it wasn't just them. Within a short space of time they learned that others, particularly those who weren't into GAA or golf, struggled to socially integrate, and that the majority no longer had any expectation that the Church would have a role there. ❧

Just as the workings of a backroom team is critical to a football or camogie club, so too is the involvement of a core group of people in parish life. They may not serve as a Parish Pastoral Council though it's to everyone's benefit that some would. Christ's vision of Christian community could never be reduced to meeting weekly for worship with a visiting priest. Nor is such worship according to the mind of God if our way of living is disconnected from the joys and hopes, grief and anguish of family, neighbours and others in our midst. If we are truly Christian then nothing that is genuinely human fails to find an echo in our hearts.[6] Often it is in our attentiveness to others, especially the poor, that we come to recognise Christ's presence in our midst.

For the past twenty years the Elphin diocese has hosted a gathering and continuing formation event for adults actively involved in voluntary Church activities of a catechetical, pastoral, liturgical and spiritual nature. Many participants present out of conviction, concern and a desire for spiritual nourishment. Twenty years ago many would have presented as a favour to their priest or in regard for the bishop's efforts to bring us into conversation. This is no longer typical of those who participate. Rather they present, in the main, because they recognise that God is calling them to play their part in building up the local Church. Their motivation is firmly grounded in their personal relationship with Jesus Christ.

The gathering is known as 'The Parish Development and Renewal Gathering' as the challenge to those who come is to bring something from it back to their parish. It's the one event, apart from meetings that I am invited to facilitate or present at, where I get opportunities to chat with clergy and officers of Pastoral Councils simultaneously. Often they travel together using the homeward journey to process the day's content. Some have served in the same or similar roles for ten years or more because they are good at what they do, well gotten by their faith communities, and in the main – 'team players'. In many cases, but not all, they have won each other's trust and admiration. They are the basis of the stability of their councils, apostolic groups and of most spin-off initiatives. It's a stability characterised by mutual respect and goodwill, seldom achieved in parishes where clergy and lay officers find themselves too busy to spend such a day together.

Keeping with the importance of stability, I would now like to introduce a Benedictine view that has much to offer Parish Pastoral Councils.

Though the number of religious in many of our dioceses continues to fall, many of us remain familiar with the practice of religious taking vows of chastity, poverty and obedience at the time of their Final Profession. These evangelical virtues are a hallmark of religious life. Final Profession for a Benedictine religious incorporates another, a vow of 'stability'.[7] It is also the practice for oblates of some Benedictine communities to undertake 'a promise of stability'. When these ceremonies are undertaken in Latin the word *stabilitas* is used and to this day there are monks, nuns and oblates who prefer to use this word when speaking of their vow or promise, suggesting its resonance is wider and deeper than our contemporary appreciation of 'stability'.[8]

So how does this speak to your heart and mine regarding the ministry of a Parish Pastoral Council? Equally importantly, how does it speak to your perception of others' sense of being a parishioner, i.e. the committed members of the faith communities that comprise our parishes?

In the introduction I emphasised that we are a Church in transition. One characteristic of this transition is that many adults under fifty years of age have opted to discontinue the practices of past generations, such as gathering with neighbours and friends on Saturday evening or Sunday morning for Mass. It comes as a complete surprise to many teenagers that churchgoers in their communities feel their absence. Their socialisation has not caused them to internalise an expectation that they would take their place in this gathering every week. There are also parishes where there hasn't been a single youth initiative in twenty years; where faith formation is deemed the preserve of the local Catholic primary school, and in some cases, where teachers are bereft of a catechising spirit or any meaningful support from the principal, Board of Management or parish.

Privately quite a number of committed Pastoral Council members have begun to question where we are going as faith communities and whether bodies like Parish Pastoral Councils have a remit regarding evangelisation and catechesis. While our parishes appear stable in so far as there is still a sizeable presence at the Sunday Eucharist or on the occasion of a funeral Mass, their ongoing viability as faith entities is not guaranteed. We can be friends and neighbours without progressing our relationship with Christ or participating in the mission of his Church. Those articulating the concern sometimes question if we are already at the end of another era of Church life and what our response should be. Would it be more prudent, for example, for us to go the route of some new ecclesial movements, discerning ways to safeguard, evangelise and catechise our own at least?

Are we making good collective decisions? This question was brought home to one Parish Pastoral Council recently when it recognised that the parish paid out on average €5,000 per annum on insurance and less than €500 on youth ministry. Others, mindful of how clubs and organisations have changed their administrative models, have begun to question if the Church needs to re-evaluate, particularly where there has been a failure to embrace developments in social media and communication. Simultaneously we are fast approaching a time in Ireland, and possibly in other parts of the Western world, when the majority of our priests will come from abroad. Is responsibility for the well-being of parish communities to be placed on their shoulders or will it, through bodies such as Parish Pastoral Councils, shift to its more rightful place, i.e. with the committed disciples of intentional Christian communities who are networked into the one parish? What considerations need to be explored in furthering such a transition?

I raise this as a sign of what may be before us and by way of illuminating that the Benedictine take on *stabilitas* never diminishes the legitimacy of such considerations, but actually embraces them. For Benedictines, to speak of stability is to speak of commitment, to sticking with something – yes, a community but primarily a community of believers. For Benedictine monks and nuns in particular it entails a lifelong vow to maintain a steady commitment of living in the spirit of the Rule, adapted to modern circumstance. It also commits each oblate to remaining affiliated with a particular monastic or convent community whilst remaining wholly committed to their specific spiritual growth context – for example, family life, employment, parish ministry – and participation in review of current structures.

Wil Derkse, a Benedictine Oblate for more than twenty years, makes the point that stability is 'not about remaining steady though you are gritting your teeth because you have obligated yourself, but rather because of the steadiness of the commitment you have given from your heart'. He writes of it as carrying on patiently and in faith, even when one is encountering a prolonged period of difficulty and/or spiritual barrenness. For him and others[9] it is remaining faithful to the Christian community or group and its ideals. It is faithfulness personified, especially when faithfulness is difficult.[10] It is also about being faithful in a manner that allows, and on occasion obligates, each oblate to examine if an adjustment or change is prudent. This is particularly the case when current arrangements, practices and relations are draining people of goodwill, energy and enthusiasm or giving rise to significant stress and strain. This can also go much deeper than adopting a principled stand. It takes a special grace in listening, one we can ask God for and prepare to receive through our commitment to active listening (see chapter three). We need God's help in order to recognise what is possible, particularly when attempting to manage a difficult work or relationship situation sensitively and creatively. The promise of stability bids us to remain positive, to endure if necessary, not in a static way but in a spiritually dynamic way that is open to the challenge of our own ongoing conversion and growth in true charity. Like the great oak that weathers many a storm during the course of its life, the oblate faces her or his difficulties in a spirit that acknowledges them as to be expected and surmountable.

Oblate poet, writer and editor Susan Sink, placed particular emphasis on the oblate's calling to pursue 'stability of heart' during her presentation at the first Oblates' World Congress in Rome in 2005. Her words are a reminder that life choices, such as whether or not to commit to the evolution of one's Parish Pastoral Council, are much more about who we are as distinct from where we are. During her presentation Sink recommended that oblates ponder the question 'How is my stability of heart?' from time to time. It's an equally good question for everyone involved in parish ministry and Church outreach. In living her oblature she discovered that her commitment to stability of heart ultimately allowed her the freedom of movement she needed to both review and make important decisions around how she was going to live. 'To be an oblate', she wrote, 'is to wake up every morning and say: "Here I am, Lord", then to walk through the day with stability of heart and focus on the values of the Rule.' Her commitment to stability ultimately found expression in living generously, especially in being welcoming of others and in maintaining a home life characterised by generosity to God (having room in her day for silence, prayer and reading the Word) and others (with whom she would spend her time).[11]

Living this way, particularly when one entwines *stabilitas* with obedience (in terms of attentive listening) and commitment to ongoing conversion of life (chapter five) can be hugely influential but also quite costly. Rowan Williams, former Archbishop of Canterbury is among those who have alluded to this. In addressing oblates during his time as archbishop he spoke of 'the danger of stability' when describing the promise to live in stability as 'the most drastic way imaginable of recognising the otherness of others – just as in marriage'.

> If the other person is there, ultimately, on sufferance or on condition, if there is a time-expiry dimension to our relations with particular others, we put a limit on the amount of otherness we can manage. Beyond a certain point, we reserve the right to say that our terms must prevail after all. Stability or marital fidelity or any seriously covenanted relation to a person, group or community resigns that long-stop possibility; which is why it feels so dangerous.[12]

Over the past twenty years I have been a member and officer of a number of pastoral groups that had fixed terms; for example, Diocesan Pastoral Council. That such groups are fixed term is as it should be. The nature of their mission is greatly enhanced through a turnover in membership. New members bring fresh energy, questions and understandings. Initial conversations between new and serving members are also laden with wonderful possibilities for growth for all … so long as leadership does not experience this as threatening or disrespectful of legitimate authority. Simultaneously I have had the experience of being a member of an apostolic organisation – The Order of The Knights of St Columbanus. We look to one another for support and encouragement as we, like countless Christians worldwide, seek to dedicate ourselves to the service of Christ in our family life, in the workplace, the marketplace and in town and provincial life. Our experience is that membership both supports and challenges us to use our resources, talents and skills to promote without imposing our Christian values and principles in our communities and society. On occasion this leads us to undertake a project together, projects that build us up as members of the body of Christ, like organising an autumn adult faith development course. At other times it is as individual members of other groups and organisations, professional, sporting, cultural, educational or political, that we seek to exert a positive influence.

Our experience suggests the collective fruitfulness of both kinds of undertaking is contingent on three things. The first is the level of conviction within our council. We have never found this to be static. It ebbs and flows and what really stands to us is having members who recognise when the tide is beginning to go out and propose we organise a nourishing input for ourselves. We have also learned that this need not be lengthy or demanding of time-poverty stricken members. A ten-minute reflection integrated into the prayer practice of our council can do wonders.

Fruitfulness can also be highly contingent on leadership styles. Certain women and men bring the best out in us. They have discerned, frequently through training, reflective exercises – for example, Ignatian examen and contemporary forms of supervision – how to foster group well-being in the service of its *raison d'être*. Good leaders are constantly building group capacity – intentionally or unintentionally. They know that positive outcomes from meetings are the fruit of good preparation, sometimes taking more time than the meeting itself. Sometimes these leaders are the officers. Other times they rightly insist on standing back so the leadership skills of others can develop.

There is also one other 'presence' in Parish Pastoral Council groupings that contributes hugely to spiritual effectiveness. Fruitfulness can also be contingent on members' commitment to their own and others' transformation in Christ through a humble docility to the Holy Spirit. Frequently these are older adults who, knowing the trials of the spiritual, now see more clearly with the eyes of the heart. They remind us to entrust everything to him who can do infinitely more than we can ask or imagine (Eph 3:20). Such members embody a holy longing quite distinct from the insatiable restlessness that has people flicking from television channel to channel or endlessly perusing social media sites and messages. They tend to present as simple and encouraging people, ministers of God's joy, never allowing negativity or setbacks to overshadow the goodness members are progressing. They also know that being oriented toward transformation in Christ does not require a council or indeed for a council to have a project or projects. Sometimes the greater challenge is to draw close to him who calls us to himself (Mt 11:28–30).

When honoured, these three considerations mentioned above – 1) Ongoing nurturing of the conviction of all members; 2) Good leadership, embracing a commitment to nurturing everyone's capacity to contribute; 3) Members' commitment to their own and others transformation in Christ through a humble docility to the Holy Spirit – have a way of dispelling the divergent visions and tensions that hold back much needed reform. They help us overcome the fears that, sometimes unknown to those of us they inhibit, manifest as arrogance and ineptitude. They are fruits of *stabilitas* on the part of one or more members, whether we use the word or not.

At the personal level, the one we can most influence, *stabilitas*, like the evangelical virtues, has the power to liberate and to open the gateway to a well-trodden pathway to greater holiness of heart. It can work to support us to be more self-emptying and in exercising a preferential love of God and neighbour. Over time, sometimes taking years, it has helped souls to recognise that it is ultimately in God that 'we live and move and have our being' (Acts

17:28). In my case, it remains very challenging, but increasingly I see its fruitfulness in groups that I am involved in. Through our struggles we are learning to be more alert and faithful to what the current moment demands and to consciously concretise where we will place our limited energies and resources. I have also had conversations with oblates whose commitment to *stabilitas* has supported their resolve to work through relationship difficulties leading, we hope, to future experiences of reconciliation. *Stabilitas* also encourages commitment to the daily mending of trust, so necessary to transformation in Christ and cooperation among his disciples. The opposite, various forms of unbounded egoism, do little good, particularly when allowed to sap the goodwill, energy and appreciation of the increasingly alienated. To promise *stabilitas* is to honour the bonds of family, fraternity and friendship, to persevere over time, rising and falling and rising again.[13]

Here in Ireland we have an expression, 'Start as you mean to go on!' Benedictines by promising 'perseverance in their stability'[14] commit to continuing as they started. The promise is deemed necessary because *stabilitas*, like *obedientia* (obedience/ attentive listening) and *conversatio morum* (daily attentiveness to conversion of heart, permanently striving to improve one's attitude and participation in community life as an expression of one's desire for union with God) do not come to us spontaneously. All three require commitment and when this is given, we mature in faith, hope and charity.

God, as Isaiah reminds us, is a 'God of tenderness and compassion, slow to anger, rich in faithful love and constancy, maintaining his faithful love to thousands, forgiving fault, crime and sin, yet letting nothing go unchecked' (Ex 34:6–7).

The invitation of the Gospel, as encapsulated in Benedictine and other well-established Christian spiritualities, is to advance toward him with confidence. Our pilgrim journey, according to the Benedictine informed mind, requires *stabilitas* and as distinguished Cistercian monk, author and abbot Michael Casey has noted, 'Stability is not a matter of immobility or resistance to change, but of maintaining one's momentum.'[15] In an era where it is easy to succumb to the paralysis of fear in the face of the excesses of unholy activism, we do well to consider what it can bring to our way of being with others. As regards our parishes and Parish Pastoral Councils it may propel us to examine and initiate conversation and dialogue around our reading of the signs of the times. Pending our personal reading of these signs, our temperament and stage of life, we may agree or disagree with the views and concerns of other members. The transmission of the faith to future generations, while primarily a grace of God, has always benefitted from human cooperation. The spirit of the Rule of St Benedict, like the Gospel on which it is modelled, is both moderate and courageous. It encourages us to take Christ at his word. He will never abandon those who, in sincerity of heart, seek to do his will.[16] Remember his many encouraging utterances to us and to those who have gone before us. For example, 'The thief comes only to steal and kill and destroy. I have come that you may have life and have it to the full' (Jn 10:10) and 'If you remain in me and my words remain in you, you may ask for whatever you please and you will get it. It is to the glory of my Father that you should bear much fruit and be my disciples' (Jn 15:7–8).

Notes

1   RB 57:9.
2   Motto of the Order of the Knights of St Columbanus, based on Eph 1:10.
3   The quotation continues: 'Why every hair on your head has been counted. So there is no need to be afraid; you are worth more than many sparrows.'
4   For example: Mt 6:26; Lk 21:18; Acts 27:34; 1 Pt 3:14; Rv 2:10.
5   This is available at: www.elphindiocese.ie/parish-pastoral-councils
6   *Gaudium et Spes, 1.*
7   RB 58:9, 17.
8   The etymology of the Latin word *stabilitas* bears out their preference. Earliest use of 'stability' in English can be traced to the mid-fourteenth century when it was used to convey both 'the firmness of resolve' and 'mental equilibrium' of individuals. Medieval French presents a slightly different take, equally illuminating. Here 'stability' is equated with 'durability and constancy'. Modern French, drawing on the Latin *stabilitatem* associates it with 'a standing fast, firmness'. From the early fifteenth century there are also descriptive usages in English expressing 'continuance in the same state'. For more on this, see: https://www.etymonline.com/word/stability. The Latin *stabilitas* encompasses them all.
9   For example, Aquinata Böckmann, *Expanding Our Hearts in Christ: Perspectives on the Rule of Saint Benedict*, Collegeville: Liturgical Press, 2005, pp. 95–96.
10 Wil Derkse, *The Rule of Benedict for Beginners*, Collegeville: Liturgical Press, 2003, pp. 22 ff.
11 Susan Sink, 'Life Choices' in Holdaway, *The Oblate Life*, pp. 60–61.
12 Rowan Williams, 'Shaping Holy Lives' in Holdaway, *The Oblate Life*, p. 149.
13 The Desert Fathers, holy men who influenced St Benedict and whose writings he recommends to us (RB 73), crafted a number of proverbs that can assist us to remember these deep spiritual truths. They include: 'A tree cannot bear fruit if it is often transplanted' and 'If a hen stops sitting on the eggs she will hatch no chickens'. Quoted in Nicholas Buxton, 'Stability' in Holdaway, *The Oblate Life*, p. 162.
14 RB 58:9–10.
15 Quoted in Buxton, 'Stability' in Holdaway, *The Oblate Life*, p. 162.
16 cf. Deut 31:6; Is 41:10; Mt 28:20; Heb 13:5.

Chapter Five

Conversatio Morum: Striving to Improve our Attitude and Engagement

In truth I tell you, unless you change and become like little children you will never enter the Kingdom of Heaven. And so, the one who makes him or herself as little as this little child is the greatest in the Kingdom of Heaven.

(Mt 18:3–4)

Just as there is a wicked zeal of bitterness which separates from God and leads to hell, so there is a good zeal which separates from evil and leads to God and everlasting life. This, then, is the good zeal which members must foster with fervent love: They should each try to be the first to show respect to the other (Rm 12:10), supporting with the greatest patience one another's weaknesses of body or behaviour, and earnestly competing in obedience to one another. No one is to pursue what they judge better for themselves, but instead, what they judge better for someone else. Among themselves they show the pure love of sisters and brothers; to God, reverent love; to their prioress or abbot, unfeigned and humble love. Let them prefer nothing whatever to Christ, and may Christ bring us all together to everlasting life.

(RB 72)

I shared earlier that Benedictine, Cistercian and Trappist monks and nuns undertake three vows at their profession: *obedientia* (attentive listening), *stabilitas* (stability, incorporating balance and moderation) and *conversatio morum* (daily attentiveness to conversion of heart, permanently striving to improve one's attitude and participation in community life as an expression of one's desire for union with God).[1] Authors experienced in living these vows, and others who have spoken of them, deem them fruitful but demanding. Benedictine Oblates who strive to adapt them to their lives agree. Within Benedictine Spirituality, *conversatio morum* is perceived as the least straightforward of the three to communicate through words over and above example.[2] It involves honouring our obligations over and above yielding to the changing feelings of each day, of striving to be open to the God-life within us, of following Christ in loving what is fragile and broken as much as what is strong, edifying and noble. It's about carrying our cross daily[3] and bringing our experiences to God in prayer, especially those that fashion, polish and temper our values, beliefs and interactions with others. It's about taking time to praise and to thank, as well as to share our needs and concerns. All Christian spiritualities have their corollaries and most of us appreciate the need for careful and periodic renovation across all aspects of life. I think in this moment of the much-loved quotation of Bernard Lonergan SJ, 'Be attentive, be intelligent, be reasonable, be responsible, and if necessary, change.' Lonergan and others were also mindful of the place of every person's choices in determining their own ongoing personal development: 'By my free acts I am making myself.' This is also characteristic of a living expression of *conversatio morum,* of cooperating in our sanctification without negating either the good or the bad of the real world around us.

As you can appreciate this is a vast topic. Here I propose to limit my engagement to two considerations:

1. How might *conversatio morum* manifest in a Pastoral Council meeting or activity to a council's or a parish's benefit?
2. How might the Benedictine understanding of *conversatio morum* help a council or an individual Pastoral Council member to take their service to the next level?

• Jack had served on the Parish Pastoral Council for five years. During that time he missed about 50 per cent of the meetings because as far as he was concerned the group had 'died and gone to heaven'! When the parish priest asked them to give one more year Jack was with the 70 per cent who expressed a wish to see elections proceed. He wanted out. The parish priest acceded but asked a final favour: 'Can each of you nominate someone and encourage them to accept your nomination?' Jack was uncomfortable and felt the need to be forthright. 'I'm sorry Fr Mick,' he said, 'but I'm uncomfortable asking. My faith is important to me but I've never felt at home at our meetings. I appreciate your homilies, your care of my mother and others who are housebound, your visits to the children in the school and I'm not trying to be offensive. You don't appear to need help with anything. I don't see the need for a council. We don't do anything.'

A stony silence followed. Jack apologised and suggested it might be best if he left. He felt he had upset everyone and was genuinely sorry. Before he got to the door, Toni spoke, 'Wait Jack. What you've said is important and you are not alone. I too have difficulties around inviting people. No offence to Fr Mick, Amanda and Paul (officers) but this (our council) isn't working!' Amanda, the chairperson, was next to speak. 'Sorry Toni and Paul. I feel responsible. You're obviously disappointed … but to be honest I have never felt that I've known enough about what we do to be chairperson.' The eyes that weren't directed to the floor were on Fr Mick. He took a deep breath, sighed and said, 'Look, honesty is important. I am grateful to all of you and I acknowledge the courage of Jack, Toni and Amanda in speaking up. Let me change my request. Could we have one more meeting, a short meeting, and could it focus on a single question – Does our parish need a pastoral council?' Eager to get away from the tension everyone readily agreed and within two minutes the meeting was wrapped up.

Jack, Toni and Amanda never perceived their sharing that night as sacred. In fact going home in their respective cars they wondered if they had been overly negative and offended Fr Mick. The reality, however, was that Fr Mick was simultaneously disappointed and pleased. He too was losing heart, fed up with the council members thinking they were there to help him and he too would be as well pleased if the council folded. Being, however, a very balanced man he found himself thinking differently within a few days. He knew the members looked to him as their spiritual leader and appreciated that. He also began to question if some good could come from the experience. ❧

Conversatio morum is at work in a number of ways in this story. Fr Mick's response is an excellent example of someone discovering in themselves a sincere and continuing effort to seek God's will in a seemingly messy and disappointing situation. The sharing of the others also serves as a powerful example of how a group can be invited to a deeper level of sharing, meaning and commitment in what might initially seem a disaster. Here integrity trumps fear and honesty paves the way for a new beginning. While our intentions are undoubtedly noble when we agree to serve on a Pastoral Council, we nevertheless need to ask periodically whether our commitment is an expression of our faith, of our love of God and neighbour, or something else? When there is no sense of the former, no debate and no call to surrender something we value – our time or another commitment – we risk superficiality, dissonance and disintegration. To quote Jack it can seem that our group 'has died and gone to heaven'!

The vicissitudes of life today are such that come evening most of us have neither the impetus nor the energy to beat around the bush. Increasingly though, we need to know – primarily for ourselves – why we have committed to a particular group, cause or undertaking. If there is a Christian dimension, then we can anticipate it will make a particular demand of us; for example, call upon us to purify our self-will, honour God's place in our lives, do our bit for others, be charitable. In others words, we experience the cost, embrace the pinch moment that tells us this is real because we also see beyond it, to a truth or truths that we know we must honour.

When a novice or an oblate joins the Benedictine community of Ampleforth Abbey, *conversatio morum* is presented to them as a vow 'to a continual change of heart, a daily reshaping of the mind and heart *according to God's plan for us*'.[4] This is something quite distinct from the urge to respond to a dramatic conversion experience or a momentary surge of compassion. One of our challenges as Christians is to recognise that our lives have a purpose or purposes for which God has equipped us. St John Henry Newman, a man who experienced the costliness of coming to the true faith, goes further and suggests we are unlikely to be satisfied until we begin to realise our purpose and potential:

> God has created me to do him some definite service. He has committed some work to me which he has not committed to another. I have my mission. I may never know it in this life, but I shall be told it in the next. I am a link in a chain, a bond of connection between persons.[5]

Equally the realisation of this sacred purpose depends greatly on the personal disposition we adopt toward it. Our efforts, for example, to be tolerant, selfless, generous and courageous are always good in themselves, but they take on additional significance when placed at the service of a greater purpose, the building up of the Kingdom of Heaven.

For centuries it was customary for Benedictine monks and nuns to interpret *conversatio morum* as underpinning their commitment to monastic life. The writings of contemporary

Benedictine religious, however, place a greater emphasis on ongoing commitment to change and to personal and group transformation.[6] The latter approach draws on the root lying behind *conversatio* meaning 'to change' or 'to be converted in the pursuit of true freedom'.

Conversatio morum reminds us not to sidestep the work of discernment that underpins all fruitful Christian activity, something essential to the workings of every Parish Pastoral Council. Every council benefits from taking time with the question 'What are we about?' Equally it can be good for us to ask of ourselves, 'What am I about as a member of this council?' At a personal level *conversatio morum* reminds us to process both our minor and major preoccupations – from what to wear to serious employment difficulties – in the light of the gospel, so as to be free to engage in mission. It supports us to redirect our energy away from thought processes and feelings that take from our participation. It challenges us to be truly present and helps us to come more readily to knowing what to do and to doing it.

When a Pastoral Council evaluates and exercises its responsibilities in similar fashion it can also lead to good outcomes. When we engage well we tend to be both caring and effective. Where changes of circumstance in our parish raise another pastoral concern, such as the closure of a factory leading to greater unemployment, we do well to discern what specific pastoral contributions we can make, and at a minimum, not contribute to the suffering of those most impacted. On other occasions, the discernment may pertain to something more contentious and less easy to articulate, such as welcoming asylum seekers of other faiths amongst us. When emotions run high and related matters are contentious, what values shall determine our contribution, if any? At such times *conversatio morum* invites us to seek the mind of Christ and to be true to his values. Such a courageous position also reminds us that our calling to be pastoral, to participate in the shepherding ministry of the Church, can bring us into conflict with others. Jesus' expression 'I have come to bring fire to the earth, and how I wish it were blazing already!'(Mt 4:19) reminds us that spiritual conflicts are neither inevitable nor unholy.

Benedictine Oblates are more fortunate than most in so far as their programmes of ongoing formation creatively and non-threateningly honour our human need to be supported in reviewing our experiences. They are unlikely to go a year or more without undertaking some review of their personal circumstance, projects and tendencies in the light of Christ's invitation to 'come follow me' (Mt 4:19) and to commit to our ongoing transformation in him in all its radicalness.[7] In promising *conversatio morum* the oblate recognises their need to attend to this more consciously and actively. She or he commits to raising in her/his consciousness and prayer their desire to be of service to God. This, of course, is by no means unique to the oblate. All who seek to be open to the influence of the Holy Spirit have a similar inkling, frequently nurtured through the contributions of clergy and catechists, through homilies, sermons, adult religious education presentations and events such as parish missions.

The sentiment of Psalm 18 also applies:

> The precepts of the Lord are right,
> they gladden the heart …
> So in them your servant finds instruction;
> great reward is in their keeping.
> But can we discern all our errors?
> From hidden faults acquit us.
> From presumption restrain your servant
> and let it not rule me. (Ps 18[19]:8, 16–17)

There is an element of discernment and follow-up to following Christ for all of us. For some of us this is supported by a regular schedule of prayer, study, some charitable work, experiences of God in silence and solitude, spiritual guidance and connection with community (which keeps us grounded). For Parish Pastoral Council members, as for oblates who are Catholic, there is also the invitation to meet with Christ in the sacraments, especially Eucharist and Penance, in the living of Holy Orders and Matrimony if one is so called, and in the scripture-based prayer with which we are encouraged to begin our meetings.

    ❧ June was thirty-three years married, a mother and grandmother, when she joined her parish's Pastoral Council. Initially she found the group's practice of reading and discussing the gospel passage of the coming Sunday 'over the top' but said nothing as some of the others liked it. She would have much preferred if they had said a decade of the rosary and invoked Our Lady's intercession. Then, one Monday night, they began to discuss the Mary and Martha story (Lk 10:38–42), the one where Jesus tells Martha that Mary has taken the better part because she takes the time to listen to him. June admitted that she could accept everything Jesus taught except that! The discussion came round to working mothers being so busy and hospitality being hard work sometimes. A younger mother on the council, conscious of the need to build community and concerned that 'church' was no longer perceived by her family as a locus of community, questioned if the Pastoral Council could oversee something that would bring people together socially without putting a huge demand on anyone? The chairperson proposed that this be put on their agenda for the next meeting and this was adopted. ❧

How does this relate to *conversatio morum*? It illustrates the good that flows from being honest with one another and the avenues of exploration that it opens up for us. Our faith doesn't just call us to turn from sin. It also calls us to celebrate life and to build community. When our listening to the word of God leads to a conversation and that conversation reveals that there are people in our community under stress and pressure, it's not enough to acknowledge them with a prayer. We need to be open, like June's council, to exploring how best to respond. This is keeping the mission of Christ before us, a mission communicated through the little stirrings in our hearts.

In my experience we (Christians) delight in the love and mercy of Christ but can be fearful or reticent because of our busyness about taking up some initiative in his name. Through his/her promise of *conversatio morum* the Benedictine Oblate publicly professes their desire to grow in holiness. Over time she or he becomes aware that this promise encompasses a commitment to play one's part in the renewal of structures and mechanisms of bodies of which they become members ... but always in the pursuit of a greater happiness and fulfilment for all. Might this also be true for Parish Pastoral Council members? What is our self-understanding of our role as members? Have we examined the priorities by which we are living and discerned where God and the mission of the Church connect with them? Are there 'sensitivities' left unspoken because others might get upset or defensive? Are we expecting leadership to come from others because we are only there because the meetings are stimulating and a nice way to pass an evening? *Conversatio morum* calls each of us to be honest with ourselves. Why? Because there is a freedom in that; a freedom that helps us and our council to move on, to attend to the pastoral issues impacting our communities. That bit of grit that is in each of us (*stabilitas*) can then more easily place itself behind our united purpose and the Holy Spirit can proceed to usher people in our direction.

Earlier we got a glimpse of a meeting that culminated with a highly significant question, 'Does our parish need a Parish Pastoral

Council?' Members with long experience of Pastoral Councils tell me that when they function according to the vision underpinning them, they tend to be excellent in outcome. When they don't, the quality of discussion deteriorates and they can become discouraging and tedious. Ask why some councils and groups appear to continually succeed, others consistently struggle and others fail miserably or fall away, and invariably the answer comes back to the goodwill, self-understanding and sense of purpose of the membership. Where there's a shared vision and openness to co-responsibility – underpinned by mutual understanding, empathy and care – growth tends to be constant. Where there's no shared vision and the attitude is that we exist to support our priest, there tends to be no tendency to critique participation or leadership, with all the pitfalls that accompany such scenarios.[8]

Great Christian spiritualities, as noted elsewhere, are pathways to holiness. None are mutually exclusive and many of their elements are drawn from the Hebrew/Old Testament and New Testament scriptures. Ultimately all seek to support women and men to enrich their personal relationship with Christ and live the Christian life. Their masters, like Christ the Master, have also been very upfront with us regarding the demands of Christian discipleship.[9] At the beginning of his Rule, St Benedict tells his reader that his message is for those 'ready to give up your own will once and for all'.[10] Christ said to his disciples, 'And indeed which of you here, intending to build a tower, would not first sit down and work out the cost to see if he had enough to complete it?' (Lk 14:26) Both sayings remain relevant today. They challenge us, particularly when we are fine with following Christ so long as he doesn't place a demand on us. And his demands may not be dramatic. As Benedictine Spirituality writer Esther de Waal has noted:

> There is no security here, no clinging to past certainties. Rather we must expect to see our chosen idols successively

broken. It means a constant letting go. It is actually, as so often in the Rule, the living out in daily life of the biblical demands, in this case St Paul's words, 'Forgetting what is behind me, and reaching out for that which lies ahead. I press towards the goal to win the prize which is God's call to the life above, in Christ Jesus' (Phil 3:13). ... What is certain is that it will involve dying, and not only death at the end of the journey but the lesser deaths in life, the dying to live, the loss which will bring new growth.[11]

June's Parish Pastoral Council went on to organise a parish social. It doubled as a fundraiser for a religious sister from the parish running a school in a poverty-stricken region of Zambia. It was a great success but also hard work for the Pastoral Council subcommittee (some members and some other parishioners who organised it). In truth they didn't realise what they were getting into. Some discussions were difficult, until they settled into the work. Then there was the anxiety as to whether people would come. However, it must also be added that they did more for the sense of belonging in the parish than any other parish initiative in the previous twenty years. The time was right for such a gathering.

Over the past fifteen years I have had a number of conversations with adults who have felt bruised by a robust exchange at a Pastoral Council meeting or by an insensitive or negative reaction to an initiative they had given much time and energy to advancing. There was an element of loss and death in the immediacy of their experience. In the reporting, however, it was not always clear that the wounding party had been deliberately confrontational, hostile or offensive or knew their words has impacted in this way. For example:

- The Altar Server Coordinator (children's ministry) who felt aggrieved when the parish priest suggested there was need to foster at least one youth ministry initiative in the parish … what did he think she was doing?

- The council member who perceived another member's suggestion that the parish could no longer afford to have weekend Masses in all three church areas as an attack on her church area, the smallest of the three.
- The Pastoral Council Parish Mission subcommittee members who felt let down because only two hundred adults participated and they had expected at least five hundred.

I would also like to share the following story.

❧ Jimmy had served on his Pastoral Council for twelve years. During that time they had raised €80,000 for parish initiatives. Meetings were monthly until the 'new' priest arrived a year ago. He had only convened two meetings and never met the officers in advance to agree an agenda. Jimmy felt very hurt when he learned the new priest had informed the Sunday congregations that he was establishing a new Pastoral Council and that he would have a guest speaker at the Masses next Sunday. What he didn't recognise or failed to notice was that their new priest had, in the past six months, spoken to every Pastoral Council member individually, including Jimmy, about pastoral initiatives he would like to introduce in the parish – for example, a Bereavement Team, organising a parish mission, a Children's Liturgy Group – and that he had encountered no enthusiasm or support. Moreover he had assumed the council were not interested in being a *Pastoral* Council as he had never had a request for any member for a meeting and in his previous parish the lay chairperson had convened all meetings. ❧

At a personal level we can all bring such experiences to our prayer but *conversatio morum* invites something more. To accept that God wants such experiences to lead 'to a continual change of heart, a daily reshaping of the mind and heart according to his plan for us'[12] invites us to explore our experience in other ways. I have been present at Pastoral Council and other Church related meetings when opposing views were expressed, sensitivities unmasked and graciously deconstructed, unforeseen consequences of past decisions teased out and failed initiatives evaluated without the apportioning of any blame. The participants knew what they were doing was difficult but remained committed because it served the common good. They also peppered their contributions with affirming comments and attentiveness to various levels of communication; for example, emotional and rational. Invariably these meetings were also characterised by other elements, for example, a time of reflective scripture-based prayer at the beginning and in one case, an established tradition of no one departing a tense meeting without first having a cup of tea together. Here, most of all, I encountered *conversatio morum* in action and not a Benedictine in sight! Here members strove to be honest, constructive and caring. Ultimately they valued the fact that members brought different viewpoints to discussions and that they were, nevertheless, the one parish. Thankfully no one was suspicious of another's motives. All recognised there was an emotional dimension to their fraternity as council members and were careful to ensure it augmented their relationship rather than undermined it.

Reflecting on their experience, and of other groups with a pastoral or apostolic mandate, I am reminded of a related observation, shared with oblates, by Archbishop Rowan Williams. He observed:

> The denial of emotion is a terrible thing; what takes time is learning that the positive path is the education of emotion, not its uncritical indulgence, which actually locks us far more

firmly in our mutual isolation. Likewise, the denial of rights is a terrible thing; and what takes time to learn is that the opposite of oppression is not a wilderness or litigation and reparation but the nurture of concrete, shared respect.[13]

This is not an invitation to unleash one's emotion on others. There are times when restraint is called for, but never to the point of denying what one is feeling or of being wholly led by a powerful feeling.

In my opening story three Pastoral Council members found the courage to communicate why they felt challenged in inviting people to take their place. By the time they were homeward bound this had evolved into being a concern as to what hurt they had caused. It's a very natural response but not necessarily a mature one. From time to time the Gospel calls on us to risk disappointment, misinterpretation, anger, fear and anxiety for the greater good. What I have gleaned is that neither the total suppression nor repression of any emotion has a positive outcome. When either occurs and important questions go unspoken, or the truth of the situation is distorted so as to keep the peace, everyone is at a loss. Tendencies to assume that others have an opposing view are equally disastrous and can dishonour a group's right to a mature dialogue. They curtail the capacity of others to make positive and valuable contributions and to utilise their skills regarding bridge- and consensus-building. Moreover they can deny the God-given aspiration in each of us toward holiness. We desire that it be honoured in us. We must work hard to ensure we honour it in others, even if there is a risk of temporary conflict. Such endeavours may take us, and particularly those of us exerting the service of leadership, into discussions that can, at least initially, be fraught with tension and distrust. But equally we must learn to trust the capacity of those we serve to reconcile at a deeper and more empowering level for our parishes. This too is a profession of our faith, a sign of our mutual respect and a commitment to

Gospel values. When our commitment to working through the various emotional, psychological and spiritual occurrences that need tending is strong, we energise one another for mission.

Equally *conversatio morum* invites us, from time to time, to explore our resistance or failure to support another group member's initiative or the resistances of council members to a suggested course of action, such as the new priest's suggestions above. Those in leadership may also support the council greatly by considering how best to honour differences of opinion. This is particularly necessary where there is support for initiatives in principle but not in practice. When others experience us as patronising they quickly cease to trust us or yield to our suggestions. Good communication is always essential.

In another context St Benedict speaks of the challenge of 'the seemingly impossible task'.[14] 'A brother or sister', he tells us, 'may be assigned a burdensome task or something he or she cannot do.' 'If so,' according to Benedict, 'she/he should, with complete gentleness and obedience, accept the order given him. Should their experience be that the weight of the burden is altogether too much for their strength, then they should choose the appropriate moment and explain patiently to their superior the reasons why they cannot perform the task. This they ought to do without pride, obstinacy or refusal. If after the explanation the superior is still determined to hold to his original order, then the junior must recognise that this is best for him or her. Trusting in God's help, he or she must in love obey.'[15]

At moments like this it is good to remember that Benedict did not foresee the many applications of his Rule that it enjoys today. What is important here are the values underpinning his advice. The nature of our consciousness today, partially shaped by an emphasis on individualism in our culture, is such that we can find ourselves believing, without examination, that certain pastoral projects are untenable in our parishes. The fact that we don't have a team of personnel, relevant infrastructure – like a centre to run a catechetics programme – can cause us to think that an issue need not be addressed. Such modes of thinking frequently mitigate against stretching ourselves and/or of seeking the counsel and support of the wider parish community. *Conversatio morum*, in such instances, may encourage a different response. What's impossible for a passionate individual or council on its own may well be in the grasp of a group who share their passion and who enjoy parish-wide support. Such mindsets underpin the wonderful advances, for example, of many sporting and cultural organisations in evolving summer camps for children. Equally they have helped evolve support forums for families challenged by various medical conditions. We are told necessity is the mother of invention, and prayer and conversation with others, sometimes help us recognise possibilities.

This is beautifully borne out in the recent publication of Ireland's National Biodiversity Data Centre, *Faith Communities: Actions to help pollinators*.[16] The National Biodiversity Data Centre is an Irish national organisation that collects and manages data to document Ireland's wildlife resources, and to track how it is changing. Through this publication, to which Fr Sean McDonagh of The Columban Ecological Institute and others had input, the Centre reminds us that we are living at a time of the sixth largest extinction of life since life began 3.8 million year ago and the tragedy of this extinction is being caused by human activity. It also reminds us that religion has great potential to change our way of relating to the earth and of the call within our faith to get to know the natural world more thoroughly and to do what we can to create a world friendly to every creature. It goes on to provide suggestions that can and have been taken up by Parish Pastoral Councils and faith communities throughout Ireland, some initiatives also doubling as youth projects.

The excellent work of these and other councils is also a reminder to us not to hold ourselves back in other ways too:

1. Holding to beliefs that a task is impossible for us.
2. Holding to a view that a pastoral need is someone else's concern.
3. Allowing feelings of inadequacy that are not of God to rule the day.
4. Failing to name our true concerns, possibly owing to a lack of courage or concern about the reaction of significant others in our lives.

What needs to be probed, according to the spirit of *conversatio morum* is our motivation and depth of vision, and our approach to discernment when we encounter a dilemma. When the Lord called the young Jeremiah to be a prophet, Jeremiah said to the Lord, 'Ah, ah, ah Lord Yahweh; you see I do not know how to speak: I am only a child!' (Jer 1:7) Jeremiah did not say no. Rather he voiced his inadequacy and inexperience, to which the Lord responded with words of encouragement and a vision that carries relevance for all of us. Later, when Jeremiah told the Lord he saw a branch of the Watchful Tree, the Lord replied, 'Well seen, for I am watching over my word to perform it' (Jer 1:12). We must grow in our appreciation of God's vigilance and as the psalmist puts it, God's desire that we 'carry out the sentence pre-ordained', an honour he holds 'for all his faithful' (Ps 149:9) (which includes us). It is very easy to be overwhelmed by fear, anxiety and negativity, particularly if the culture of our group tends to magnify our awareness of our limitations. When this happens our council may be reduced to a periodic social get-together. *Conversatio morum* invites us to look at ourselves and our community as a whole with fresh eyes; eyes that see what we have as distinct from what we do not have.

Here too the thrust of St Benedict's Rule offers encouragement tempered with wisdom, i.e. to always approach *conversatio morum* in a balanced manner. The Benedictine way invites the monk, nun, oblate and Parish Pastoral Council member to be proportionate and respectful of their and others' human limitations, bodily and spiritual. Excessive zeal and every form of reactionary response to a new realisation regarding the dynamics, etc. of our councils, meetings and projects are to be tempered with an equal commitment to *stabilitas* (stability incorporating balance and moderation) and *obedientia* (attentive listening). While undertaking the work of conversion is good for us, both as individuals and groups, we should also foster a certain contentment with the familiar, the ordinary, mindful that 'we are essentially rhythmic creatures, and that life needs this rhythm and balance if it is to be consistently good and not drain from us the precious possibility of being or becoming our whole selves'.[17]

As Christians we are encouraged to review our lives periodically. This excellent practice supports us in hearing God's word and in being true to our faith. Could there also be a value in adopting mechanisms to support us to review our council meetings and activities? At the beginning of this chapter I included St Benedict's observation that there is 'a good zeal which separates from evil and leads to God and everlasting life'.[18] I preceded it with Christ's teaching that unless we change and become like little children we will never enter the Kingdom of Heaven (Mt 18:34). Taken together they remind us that conversion of heart also involves letting go, of creating spaces as children do for others to join them in their enterprises. Another teaching of Jesus' is equally pertinent: 'If anyone wants to be a follower of mine, let him renounce himself and take up his cross and follow me' (Mk 8:34). Christ continues to speak these and similar words to every disciple through the ministry of the Church; for example, 'Anyone who wants to save his life will lose it; but anyone who loses his life for my sake, and for the sake of the gospel, will save it' (Mk 8:35–36). Here Christ alludes to the challenge of deep conversion which goes some way to explaining the turbulences and tensions that frequently accompany genuine spiritual growth. In this context *conversatio morum* emboldens us not to be discouraged by tensions arising from differences of opinion, interpersonal difficulties, etc. Our shared commission to evangelise, catechise and play our part in building up our faith communities is likely to draw on the breath of our acquired competencies and contribute to their purification. This is part and parcel of being alive in Christ.

It, as Benedictine Oblates may testify, may also necessitate an honouring of the practical demands of our faith. St Benedict is very strong on matters such as the distribution of goods according to need, the care of the sick, of the elderly and children and of hospitality towards guests, including unwanted guests.[19] His Rule incorporates no less than seventy-three short, snappy injunctions under the striking heading 'The Tools for Good Works'.[20] Here every Benedictine monk, nun and oblate and all who draw inspiration from him are reminded to live biblical prescripts such as honour everyone (1 Pt 2:17), never do to another what you do not want done to yourself (Tob 4:16), never act in anger or nurse a grudge, never give a hollow greeting of peace or turn away when someone needs your love, never repay a bad deed with another (1 Th 5:15), bear injustice patiently (Lk 6:27), do not grumble or speak ill of others (RB 4:40), remember the Lord's teaching 'Do what they say, not what they do' (Mt 23:3), do not aspire to be called holy before you really are, do nothing out of envy, and never lose hope in God's mercy.[21] According to Benedict these are the 'tools of our spiritual craft', for which our reward when we return them on judgement day, will be 'What no eye has seen and no ear has heard, what the mind of man or woman cannot visualise; all that God has prepared for those who love him!' (1 Cor 2:9) Over the years a number of Parish Pastoral Councils have found innovative ways of honouring them. My favourite concerns a parish that entered a twinning arrangement with a parish in the developing world, one where poverty causes immense suffering. I was particularly impressed with reports that indicated council members went beyond giving money and other supplies and took time to create and nurture relationships with people in their twin parish.

Elsewhere in his Rule – for example, chapter six 'Restraint of Speech' and chapter seven 'Humility' – Benedict is very explicit regarding the life we are called to and the commitment the Gospel seeks. Not one to beat around the bush he is particularly virulent regarding all forms of Christianity characterised by a lack of attentiveness toward God and divine things, or laziness or aloofness regarding love of one's neighbour. Our calling to cooperate with God must not be reflected in inaction, a lack of genuine charity and, in the Pastoral Council context, inappropriately curtailed discussions or failure to expand an agenda to attend to the needs of others. In all of this, however, we must remember we are never alone. As women and men admitted to God's favour[22] we must learn to work out of the love God has poured into our hearts by the Holy Spirit. Striving to improve our attitudes and engagement is a response to his presence in our lives. We come to this work as beloved adopted children of God, called to share in his building up of his Kingdom. Perseverance is called for in the face of hardship but Christ will not be overcome. Our 'yes' to serving on a Pastoral Council is not without foundation. Perhaps we have had some personal experience of God's unconditional love, and deep within us, we are seeking to return love for love.[23] Perhaps such an experience has not yet been ours. Either way, I anticipate all of us know what it is to be uplifted by experiences of kindness, charity, forgiveness, healing and redemption. Equally we probably know what it is to be tested by the harshness, rejection, fear and control emanating from our own and others' sinfulness and woundedness. The gospel invitation is never to reject where we have come from or where we have been, but in the love of Christ to transcend our difficulties so that we and others have a better life. The call is to be our authentic human selves.

The honesty that *conversatio morum* requires is, I believe, more easily sustained when we can be humble before God together. Humility is a quality, in my experience, characteristic of true friendship.[24] When friends are accepting and non-judgemental, when we can present our wounded and flawed natures to one another as easily as our joys, we facilitate each other to grow spiritually, emotionally, psychologically and caringly. Some friendships and acquaintanceships also draw oblates and Parish Pastoral Council members to new horizons, causing us to delve more deeply into the mystery of our faith. We can find ourselves needing to attend to something quite unexpected, and all the time need to be asking 'Where is God in all of this?' A final story by way of example:

🙠 Mandy came to live in St Ignatius' parish five years ago with her partner Brian and their daughter Micheala. Every weekday morning she dropped into the church to light a candle by way of invoking God's blessing on her day. She avoided the church on Sunday mornings as she understood from comments of colleagues at work that divorcees weren't welcome. Jack, her boss, a member of the Pastoral Council got wind of this and was very disturbed by it. Mandy was a very honest and dependable worker and the first to reach for her purse when there was a fundraiser. She didn't discriminate against anyone. This couldn't be right he thought! Without naming Mandy or drawing attention to her, he raised his concern at the next Pastoral Council meeting. 'Should the council encourage Catholics who are staying away because they are divorced, to come to Mass?' He was quite surprised and irked when one third of the council communicated the council could not condone divorce. There were also those who said they and other parishioners would be fine with it so long as the divorcees hadn't entered second relationships. Emotions ran high and discussion became quite heated. Jack found himself asking, 'But surely everyone who seeks to live the Christian life as best they can is welcome to join us at Mass?' The replies indicated that there wouldn't be any consensus that night so the chairperson adjourned the discussion.

Next day I got a call from Fr Thaddeus, the parish priest. 'What is your own view,' I queried? 'Of course they are welcome but as a pastor I'm concerned that this could become divisive and lead to further hurt and alienation. One of my questions is "How can I introduce the Pastoral Council and others to the current discipline of the Church regarding such situations?" The fact that it is not black and white will go hard on some of them.' We agreed to chat again a week later, committing ourselves to rereading in the meantime the relevant sections of Pope Francis' 2016 Post-Synodal Apostolic Exhortation *Amoris Laetitia* (The Joy of Love)[25] and the 2015 *Final Report of the Synod of Bishops on the Vocation and Mission of the Family in the Church and in the Contemporary World*.[26] We found that both documents affirmed Fr Thaddeus' heartfelt desire to be a loving pastor to all. We also noted the Church's pastoral sensitivity to people in second unions, and the encouragement of priests, when pastoral opportunities arose, to engage with Catholics in second unions in a discernment to see whether or when the reception of Holy Communion at Mass may be appropriate.

Furthermore, as Jack was known to me and I knew him to be a very good person, I encouraged Fr Thaddeus to speak with him. In this way he learned about Mandy. Being a skilled pastor he arranged his timetable so as to cross paths with Mandy and over a few weeks got to know her. She appreciated this very much. She was also delighted when Fr Thaddeus asked her if she had ever considered joining the choir and the first Sunday she sang with them Jack and his wife Mary lingered after Mass to chat with her about the experience. To this day Mandy has no idea of what she ignited in Jack and how this links with Fr Thaddeus' invitation to join the choir. ❧

That Pastoral Council continues to discuss this and other pastorally sensitive topics. Discussions are easier now in the sense that members are more accustomed to such discussions … and they have learned to agree to disagree. In each instance Fr Thaddeus communicates the Church's teaching and frequently draws on the writings and homilies of Popes Francis, Benedict and John Paul II in encouraging each member to be pastorally sensitive to all parishioners. If he senses that a member's contribution is rooted in a story or concern relating to a parishioner or family member he tends to make his own discreet enquiries and in each case people have valued his contact, pastoral concern, care and discretion.

I share this story as an example of a 'conversion' issue where there is never likely to be uniformity of opinion among Catholic Christians. In two thousand years there has never been a time when all women and men's life experiences, the Church's teaching and the broader Church's pastoral response were in sync. To acknowledge this is not sinful. We do well to recognise that convictions around matters such as divorce, homosexuality, birth control and gender identity can be formed by many variables and the more personal they are, the stronger a person's conviction is likely to be. What *conversatio morum* puts before us – both individually and collectively – is a call to moderation in our pastoral response. We must practise temperance, which often incorporates continence. At the time St Benedict wrote his Rule chronic disorder was giving rise to much suffering. In his desire to create environments (monastic communities) in which order ruled he encouraged practical discretion and took care to ensure that the demands placed on his monks were not excessive and thereby counterproductive. To remember that God is love, that he is present and working in each of us according to his plan and purposes, is important. We do well when like Fr Thaddeus we offer those who believe themselves to be on the margins opportunities to experience the fellowship of the Lord with us. We need not be judge and jury, while at the same time reserving and retaining the right to communicate the Church's teachings and the premises on which they stand.

Ultimately Benedictine Spirituality, like the Gospel on which is it grounded, invites us to forgo complete reliance on our personal capacities and competencies and to yield to the benevolent influence of the Holy Spirit as he leads us into deeper ways of loving God and our neighbour. For many of us, God's invitation to trust encompasses an adjustment of our modes of thinking, allowing the light of the Gospel access, and giving expression to this through attitudinal adjustments and small improvements, such as lessening our carbon footprint, inviting others to share their views and tolerating them when we don't like them, and most importantly, taking time to communicate our challenges to God. We come to recognise ourselves as good but flawed, as possessing a blind side. If we are fortunate we also come to recognise that it is only through Christ that all evil can be changed to good, including the evil in ourselves. Esther de Waal put it succinctly when she wrote, 'Grace evokes our acts, supports them and fulfils them.'[27] Our primary task, at many levels, is acceptance of the teaching contained in the gospel passage that opened this chapter (Mt 18:1–5), to make ourselves as little children, trusting of God, making his law our delight and pondering it day and night.[28]

Both the concluding chapters of St Benedict's Rule and salvation history convey our Lord's very warm consideration for human weakness.[29] The lifelong process of being transformed in Christ, of coming to spiritual, psychological and emotional maturity in him, should not frighten us. Rather we should strive to take Benedict's advice to heart, 'And finally, never lose hope in God's mercy.'[30]

Each day Benedictines throughout the world pray, *Suscipe me Domine* ('Uphold me, O Lord'), mindful of their weakness and God's greatness. It is the prayer of many others too as they face weighty challenges. It can also be the prayer of the Parish Pastoral Council member who, despite personal shortcomings and sinful tendencies, continues to desire to be among those St Benedict identified when he wrote: 'Let them prefer nothing whatever to Christ, and may he bring us all together to everlasting life.'[31]

Notes

1   The vows are based on RB 58:17 and a number of English translations of the Rule translate *conversatio morum* as 'fidelity to the monastic life'.

2   Terrence Kardong OSB and other RB historians and scholars note that soon after the time of Benedict, some scribes began changing *conversatio to conversio,* which can be translated literally as 'conversion' (see Terrence Kardong OSB, *Benedict's Rule: A Translation and Commentary,* Collegeville: Liturgical Press, 1997, p. 483 ff.). This misrepresentation came to light in 1912 through the work of another distinguished Benedictine scholar, Abbot Cuthbert Butler OSB. While the exact meaning of *conversatio morum suorum* remains subject to slightly different shades of meaning, there is a general consensus that it pertains to continuing fidelity to the monastic/intentional Christian life. In this sense it is broader than 'conversion of heart', conveying also a commitment to 'frequency' and 'conversation' in the modern English sense.

3   cf. Mt 16:24–26.

4   See: https://www.ampleforth.org.uk/abbey/our-life/vows

5   John Henry Newman, 'Some Definite Service' from *Meditations and Devotions,* Part III, 'Hope in God—Creator (2)', 1848. Available at: http://www.newmanreader.org/works/meditations/meditations9.html#doctrine1

6   For example, Chittister, Casey, Pennington, Böckmann and oblates, Derkse, Scrubas, Longenecker and Vest.

7   cf. Mt 16:24–26.

8   One such pitfall relates to the challenge of renewing the council at the end of its term. Young adults in particular can find it very difficult to recommit where the culture of the council fails to embrace decision-making, planning and experimentation. The absence of an outlet for their goodwill can leave them with the view that the council is rather a matter for older adults.

9   cf. Mt 7:13, 22:14; Lk 6:26, 14:26–27.

10 RB, Prologue, 3.

11 Esther de Waal, *Seeking God: The Way of St Benedict,* Norwich: Canterbury Press, 1999, p. 70.

12 Ampleforth Abbey definition quoted earlier.

13 Rowan Williams, 'Shaping Holy Lives' in Holdaway, *The Oblate Life,* p. 152.

14 RB 68.

15 Ibid.

16 National Biodiversity Data Centre, *Faith Communities: Actions to help pollinators – All Ireland Pollinator Plan, 2015–2020.* Available at: https://pollinators.ie/wordpress/wp-content/uploads/2018/08/Faith-Communities_actions-to-help-pollinators-2018-WEB.pdf

17 de Waal, *Seeking God: The Way of St Benedict,* p. 93.

18 RB 72.

19 RB 34, 36, 37, 74, 4.

20 RB 4.

21 RB 4:74.

22 cf. Rm 5:1–6.

23 cf. Rm 12:1–2.

24 I will return to this in chapter seven.

25 Pope Francis, *Amoris Laetitia*. Available at: https://w2.vatican.va/content/dam/francesco/pdf/apost_exhortations/documents/papa-francesco_esortazione-ap_20160319_amoris-laetitia_en.pdf

26 Synod of Bishops, *Final Report of the Synod of Bishops on the Vocation and Mission of the Family in the Church and in the Contemporary World*. Available at: http://www.vatican.va/roman_curia/synod/documents/rc_synod_doc_20151026_relazione-finale-xiv-assemblea_en.html

27 de Waal, Seeking God, p. 78.

28 cf. Ps 1.

29 cf. RB 72, 73; Is 40:29; Ps 73:26; Mt 11:28; 1 Pt 5:7; Phil 4:13; Rm 8:26.

30 RB 4, 74.

31 RB 72.

Chapter Six

Leadership and Authority: Sustaining Fruitful and Workable Arrangements

No, anyone who wants to become great among you must be your servant, and anyone who wants to be first among you must be your slave, just as the Son of Man came not to be served but to serve, and to give his life as a ransom for many.

(Mt 20:26–28)

'He is to distrust his own frailty and remember not to crush the bruised reed (Is 42:3). By this we do not mean that he should allow faults to flourish, but rather, as I have already said, he should prune them away with prudence and love as he sees fit for each individual. Let him strive to be loved rather than feared.'

(RB 64:13–15)

In the introduction I mentioned this book has been written particularly for women and men who exert a service of leadership in and through their Parish Pastoral Council. I noted that when we are good enough to commit to a Parish Pastoral Council, parish project or initiative we like to see it realise positive outcomes. Councils are now coming into prominence and where a spirit of co-responsibility characterises the relationship between parish priest and other members, there is great potential. We come to our councils as unique individuals, each with a personal and unique story. For this reason, previous chapters have sought to support readers review their own spiritual context, principally by drawing on elements of Benedictine Spirituality. My aspiration was to assist everyone see their own life and ministry in the light of the gospel more clearly. With this chapter comes a change of focus. It aspires to support you consider the service you and others offer as Parish Pastoral Council members and how best to render it. It is also underpinned by a question: 'Where does authority reside regarding the matters being explored in this book?'

One of the blessings of my life is frequent contact with Parish Pastoral Council members across many parishes. I know many as women and men of deep and abiding faith; a faith frequently, joyfully and charitably expressed at parish level. The majority are also busy people; rearing families, holding down jobs, exercising other voluntary commitments in their communities. The pathways by which we have come to know each other are significant. In the main they have been fourfold:

1. Through diocesan opportunities to nurture our understanding of the faith, such as coming together to explore Pope Francis' encyclical *Laudato Si'* (On Care for our Common Home).
2. Through pre-sacramental programmes aimed at supporting parents and grandparents prepare their children for the sacraments of Penance, First Holy Communion and Confirmation.
3. Through Church ministry formation programmes and review meetings, such as gatherings with Parish Pastoral Council members, choirs, Minister of the Words, Extraordinary Minister of the Eucharist.
4. Chatting when our paths cross unexpectedly.

These occasions have provided us with opportunities to explore what's happening around us and how the Gospel is tugging at us to respond. Those of us who exert a service of leadership know it as something at times difficult to negotiate in practice. Our fellow members and others frequently communicate an awareness of the same challenges; for instance, supporting our young people to come to faith or how best to reach out to the disaffiliated. Where we can feel challenged is in working out what our personal and community responses need to be. Experienced leaders tend to be quieter than others during such discussions. When they do speak, their contributions tend to confirm something well enunciated in Benedictine and other Christian spiritualities – that Gospel-based servant leadership can sometimes be unsettling. They often note how challenging it is to encourage anything that it is countercultural, including faith practice.

ᔕ I recall a time when Fr Manus offered a delightful nugget of encouragement to a deanery gathering of Parish Pastoral Council chairpersons and secretaries, very pertinent to the overall aim of this chapter. He contrasted his experience of introducing the Ministry of Extraordinary Minister of the Eucharist forty years ago with the relative ease with which present-day Pastoral Council members assist their priests to recruit Ministers of Holy Communion to bring the Eucharist to housebound parishioners. Forty years ago many lay people found it difficult to transition to receiving Holy Communion from a fellow lay person. Accustomed to distribution being reserved to clergy, they questioned the validity and thinking behind the change. According to Fr Manus it took time and lots of good communication, listening and teaching, listening again and teaching again. Once understood, accepted and established as the new norm, subsequent changes were much easier to introduce but still required good communication. ᔕ

In my experience most of us, once our priority commitments allow, quite enjoy being of assistance to others but we recoil a little when asked to lead or exert authority. This is not surprising. Being a leader or part of a leadership group asks more of us and it's one of the reasons resources tend to be directed to leaders. In Ireland, Parish Pastoral Councils have been particularly fortunate in the good work of the Irish Catholic Bishops' Conference's Council for Pastoral Renewal and Adult Faith Development. Over the past two decades it has published a number of strategic resources aimed at supporting the self-understanding and mission of all Pastoral Council members. These documents are the fruit of much lived experience distilled through relevant Church teaching and mindful of present needs.

In the most pivotal of them, *Living Communion: Vision and Practice for Parish Pastoral Councils Today*, Pastoral Councils are recognised as leadership groups through which priests and laity 'work together as partners in fulfilling the mission of Christ in their own place'.[1] There is a strong emphasis throughout on visioning the Church as a communion with Christ at the centre. The document also offers an informed understanding of 'parish', one cognisant of the need for future collaboration both in and between parishes. It also provides the reader with the canonical basis of Parish Pastoral Councils and a summary statement of their role and function within parishes. Suggested and well-conceived guidelines for the setting up of new councils are also offered and these are followed by the identification of excellent processes that councils can utilise to support their effectiveness. Methods of ongoing review and evaluation are also offered and encouraged, along with ongoing formation suggestions.

Many dioceses have followed up by developing training initiatives and opportunities to support new Pastoral Council members. A cohort of these, having previously served on Parish Councils tend to highlight the transition from 'maintenance' to 'mission'. Today we are encouraged to be more concerned about the people than the plant that serves the people. These training opportunities have also sought to illuminate the kind of leadership Parish Pastoral Councils are being invited to exert. Generally they place particular emphasis on the importance of leading in such a way as to 'bring the parish with you'. Such opportunities have also been consolidated in some dioceses through review, renewal and ongoing training events; for expamle, an in-service day for chairpersons and secretaries. A key phrase, sometimes laboured, is 'servant leadership in a spirit of co-responsibility'. This necessitates that clergy and councils come to a shared vision, one that necessitates a certain letting go for priests and a certain taking up for laypersons. It requires that we grow confident in communicating with each other, articulating our questions and expectations, and mutually clarifying our understanding of our role as Parish Pastoral Council members.

How is this going nationally? I am not aware of any studies but anecdotal evidence suggests a number of councils are beginning to find their feet and to thrive. It is good too to note that parishes are not alone at this time in evolving new forms of leadership. Recent decades have seen almost every religious community in Ireland take time to reflect and to evaluate its leadership model. This is beautifully reflected in the appendices of *Living Communion: Vision and Practice for Parish Pastoral Councils Today*. Here readers are introduced to elements of discernment processes that support both the formation and workings of Parish Pastoral Councils. The writers, all highly experienced in supporting pastoral councils, have drawn on the experience of religious communities. They are also to be commended for the continuity between this and another contribution from the Irish Bishops' Conference, *Share the Good News: National Directory for Catechesis in Ireland* (2010). Regarding leadership and authority this is particularly significant at the level of recognising layers of responsibility and possibility:

1. It recognises that contemporary challenges call for the further education, training and payment at appropriate levels of committed lay people ... 'if we wish to offer coming generations the Good News we have been given'.

2. It urges individual Catholics to take responsibility for their personal faith education, both for their own good and for that of their community.
3. It identifies the parish community as the focal point of faith development going forward.[2]

The Directory states: 'A fully formed and empowered Church community, guided by the Holy Spirit, will have so much to say, in union with Jesus Christ, for our world today.'[3] The journey to being 'full formed and empowered', however, is a lengthy one. Benedictine Spirituality, as we shall see later, also advocates the need to face related challenges collaboratively. Though the Directory places responsibility for the local advancement and fostering of catechesis, in keeping with canon law, firmly in the barrow of the parish priest (pp. 190–196), it's difficult to envisage any progression without Parish Pastoral Council support. This brings me to the three-fold thesis of this chapter:

1. The effectiveness of Pastoral Councils, as expressions of co-responsibility between priests and parishioners, are contingent on evolving relationships of trust sufficiently robust to accommodate today's pastoral landscape.
2. Means need to be found to share ownership of pastoral priorities with the parish at large.
3. Movement to such a position needs to be Christ- and person-centred and would do well to draw on the riches of Christian spiritual traditions such as Benedictine Spirituality.

Over the past decade greater numbers of Pastoral Council members have begun to question how parishes can support evangelisation and catechesis. New initiatives, like running an Alpha course, have worked very well in helping councils to see what can be involved and what is meant by evangelisation and catechesis.[4] Such opportunities, initially, are often contingent on the willingness of one or two members' goodwill, energy and competencies. They tend to be greatly encouraged when councils evolve to having 'evangelisation and catechesis' as standing items on monthly agendas. For many lay leaders and clergy this is new ground, an innovation toward mission. It can feel a bit strange initially as we are not accustomed to talking with one another in this way. Simultaneously this evolution, fragile and fragmented at times, is key to a council's pastoral identity. These discussions are helping us to recognise our remit. We find ourselves learning new words and talking more freely about the renewal of our parishes as faith communities. Evolving sustainable models of parish catechesis remains challenging, however, particularly where few clergy and officers have the heart for what it entails. When this is the case councils are often contingent on the leadership of members who are not officers. What is most important though is that no one loose heart or feel they are in the wrong place. The Holy Spirit is leading us to a new horizon.

In a very real sense we are in transition and co-responsibility through Parish Pastoral Councils is being encouraged going forward. So where are we in terms of this transition and might there be merit in identifying where leadership and authority currently reside in our parishes and Parish Pastoral Councils? Is it, for example, with the parish priest? Is it with the council or key individuals within our council? Is it with the parish ... or with what we think people think? Is it with the Pope or the local bishop when he speaks on a matter that concerns us? In my experience, even when councils undertake the development of a mission statement and sign up to an agreed vision, significant variances of perception remain. Sometimes this is further exacerbated by differing perceptions as to what 'leadership' and 'authority' are. The idealist in each of us is frequently inspired by definitions like that of Anselm Grün OSB:

To lead means first of all to arouse people to life, to entice life out of them. Leading is the art of finding the key which can open the treasury of your co-worker.[5]

There is a danger here of oversimplification. Leadership, particularly servant leadership, cannot be reduced to getting other people to do what we want them to do. Grün goes on to speak about it being much more than saying the right word at the right time. He acknowledges the importance of encouraging conversation, allowing for personality considerations, time constraints and assumptions as one supports the building of trust, so essential to solid pastoral, catechetical and evangelical outcomes.

❧ When Fr Michael was appointed parish priest it came as no surprise to his brother priests that he wanted the Pastoral Council to assist him to run an autumn adult faith development programme in the parish centre. Fortunately he took on board that his predecessor or previous councils had never tried anything of this nature. At his first Pastoral Council meeting he asked the group if they would be willing to share their thoughts on a fifteen-minute video presentation the next time they met. All were delighted. This was new and life-giving. The video, produced to a very high standard, focussed on the Sacrament of Penance and the members found it very enriching. Fr Michael shared that he had another on the Eucharist that he would be happy to share at the next meeting but he suggested they curtail the time allotted to it to twenty minutes so as not to deflect from their other business. Again all agreed. Only after the council had had both experiences did he query if some members would be willing to form a subcommittee with him to offer such experiences to parishioners. He then got four volunteers, all looking forward to helping out … because they could appreciate what was involved and the potential outcomes. ❧

I, and others, share a liking for the etymology of words with Fr Michael. 'Authority' and 'leadership' are particularly interesting. Stemming from the Latin *auctoritas*, 'authority' communicates 'support or power conferred, particularly by way of helping to grow and give increase'. Note how Fr Michael shared his authority with the council. In the broadest sense we may think of the authority, for example, by which an authoritative book settles an argument among scholars. The word also carries overtones of 'capacity building', particularly of people through teaching, offering advice or a well-informed opinion.

Some Benedictine writers have also illuminated its significance in other ways. For example, Norvene Vest has written about 'authority' as carrying connotations of 'originator' and 'source', going right back to the source of all that is good, the One from whom all abundance flows (Jas 1:17). For her and others 'to be under authority' is to be under a benevolent and powerful influence. Put more simply, she invites us to see God working for our benefit in and through others, by contributing to our deliberations and undertakings.

The etymology of 'leadership' is also quite interesting. It draws on the Old English word *laedere* and Middle English word *-schipe*. *Ladere* is a noun referring to one who leads, one who is first, the one who is most prominent and charged with guiding or conducting. *-Schipe* is a word-forming element with the connotation of 'state or condition of being'.[6] Applied to the contemporary Pastoral Council context, there is no doubt regarding the relevance of both concepts and of their overlapping nature. What, however, are our indicators of successful realisation to be? The American writer and political commentator, Walter Lippman, is attributed with the line, 'The final test of a leader is that they leave behind them in others the conviction and the will to carry on.' Let us think for a moment of persons who inspired us to commit to something other than ourselves and who are no longer with us. What was it about them that enlivened our spirits in a manner that got us beyond our inhibitions or other priorities? Is there something to be mined here, something that may colour how we exercise pastoral leadership authoritatively?

Another striking characteristic of Benedictine monastic leadership, that is applicable in our parish contexts, is its intentionality. Benedictine communities are intentional communities and this is reflected in the styles of leadership adopted. Their shared intentions both shape and orient every Benedictine monastic community and the various arrangements – including oblation – that emanate from the Benedictine way of life. Though parish life is much more diverse we share with these monastic communities a commitment to the Gospel. Like monks, nuns and oblates, we too can access through adapted forms of St Benedict's Rule, a Gospel-inspired pathway to holiness of life. It's something we can turn to when a new or pervading challenge presents itself.

One of the challenges St Benedict foresaw besetting some monastic communities was seeing beyond the immediacy of what needed to be tended to.[7] He recognised the service of leadership as having a broader emphasis. Our Parish Pastoral Councils can also benefit from taking a short- and long-term view, mindful that expediency sometimes detracts us from seeing 'the big picture'. We are fortunate when officers and other leaders facilitate us to enquire, dialogue and reach consensus around short- and long-term goals, ensuring linkages with 'the continual becoming' of the faith communities that comprise our parishes. Thus servant leadership extends much further than calling a meeting to order and ensuring the agenda is expedited. There is more to these roles than the utilisation of leadership techniques in the service of agreed projects. Creating a climate and culture that builds engagement capacity is vital. Part of this is giving time to discerning questions to support meaningful discussion. It is also keeping an eye to our eternal destiny.[8]

Those who have written about related matters from a Benedictine perspective – for example, Chittister, Vest, Wolf or Olivera – consistently emphasise the necessity for those in leadership to develop a distinct attitude regarding people, authority, relationships and work, one quite different from those associated with the success–failure paradigms rampant in corporate circles. These authors are equally consistent in advocating that such attitudes are challenging to achieve. Leaders, in their view, must avoid the temptation of becoming caught up in managing relations, finances or Mass time schedules, and keep an ear attuned to the heartfelt concerns of community members. It is easier for people to engage with us when they know we care for them and ultimately that is what Christ wants of us. How we treat one another, the respect we accord one another is much more significant than any structural reform we may need to address.

The emphasis on leadership in the Rule of St Benedict clearly communicates his awareness of the power of leadership to make or break, to foster confidence or, left unchecked, to utterly undermine it.[9] It honours the importance of choosing people with the relevant dispositions and competencies[10] and everyone's desire and need to be treated graciously.[11] It also honours our need to both identify and clarify expectations: 'So why have I committed to the Pastoral Council?' These realisations of St Benedict are more commonly understood today but it is good for us to apply them to the Pastoral Council context. When people participate in any meeting they like to know who is in charge, the protocols that will be followed and that the dignity of all members will be upheld. When the chairperson, for example, takes their cue from another member such as the parish priest, all can readily see that their role, whilst certainly one of service, is not authoritative.[12] Indeed the evolution of leadership within and by Pastoral Councils may be both served and complicated by the varying expressions of priesthood laity encounter at parish level. The pastoral nature of the priestly ministry and its manifestation through the individual personality of each priest means we will never have 'a one size fits all' scenario. Nor need that be a concern once our capacity to review together becomes well established. Priests rightly have concerns regarding their responsibilities, pastoral and fiscal, and there are never grounds for a Pastoral Council to work against these. Notwithstanding it is good when leadership, clergy and lay, unite behind a dedicated desire to explore and further the mission of Christ in the parish in a spirit of co-responsibility. Then much can be achieved.

Thankfully the fruits of the current movement toward co-responsibility are becoming more apparent in parishes, but I think it is also true to say that they are equally dependent on individuals, voluntary and professional, who advance approved initiatives. A plethora of developments including RCIA programmes run according to the spirit of the rite, parish youth initiatives, social gatherings, improved communications with parishioners via parish websites and social media, are increasingly pervasive, but in many instances, supported by the good work of parish pastoral workers, catechists and deacons. Pastoral Councils have exercised a fruitful role in birthing many such developments but they rightly take on a life of their own. Informed by open conversation, feedback and consequent goodwill, such developments have contributed to a revitalisation of ailing parishes. Having identified the distinction between leadership and management and responsibility for initiating and maintaining, they more readily support sustainable and viable approaches to pastoral development.

Management, the rightful concern of parish priests and bodies such as Parish Finance Committees, rightly tends to important administrative and maintenance concerns, some of which, while requiring the oversight of a group, rarely require group action. Effective leadership on the other hand, as St Benedict and the Benedictine tradition present it, is rather in the business of illuminating, energising and building capacity (I will present some examples shortly). And how much easier it is for a leadership group, such as a Pastoral Council, to energise when it is successfully invigorated by its own leadership. How powerful it is when individuals and groups actively support and encourage their membership to stretch themselves beyond where past experience has led them, particularly in the service of connecting with the broader parish community. Perhaps too the time has come to ask ourselves, if in our present way of being with one another, we are sufficiently honouring God's presence among us, and the charisms we have received from the Holy Spirit?

Sadly, there are council members for whom all of the above shall seem quite distant, members for whom experiences of meetings are few and far between and when they do occur, they may secretly question their own presence: 'Why am I here?' They may also have experience of meetings where participants' states of mind never lent themselves to engaging with a meaningful topic or proposing a course of action that energised the group or conveyed genuine interest in or care of others. An application of the wisdom of Benedict to such scenarios requires us to go no further than the opening lines of the Rule. Early on he warns of the power of 'the sloth of disobedience' and its power to draw us away from Christ, or the life Christ wishes for us and the mission we have been invited to accomplish.

Where a pastoral group or its leadership find themselves unable to engage in meaningful conversation or undertake a significant spiritual or pastoral action, or have become characterised by disinterestedness, complacency and spiritual torpor, something is amiss. The challenge is more deeply rooted than the animation of the meeting. According to Benedict (by implication) such groups are on a downward spiritual spiral, rooted in disobedience, the root of most of our major difficulties. Here too we must remember that Benedict was writing in the sixth century. Contemporary commentators remind us that the word 'disobedience' has a different connotation today. Vest alludes to the connectivity between disobedience and the etymology of the word 'absurdity', drawing from the Latin words *ab-surdus,* meaning to be stone-deaf to something, deaf to its meaning.[13] Boulding, on the other hand, suggests overtones of laziness and failure to engage, while Derkse links it with the spiritual inertia and resistance to conversion many of us encounter more often that we care to admit.[14]

Here too it is good to remember that St Benedict speaks as a loving father, one familiar with human capabilities and weaknesses, mindful that God is at work in each of us, desiring to bring his will to completion in us.[15] Though our society differs significantly from his, many would argue that human nature has not dramatically altered over the past 1,500 years.

Another story, this time from another diocese, to help contextualise some of this teaching:

❧ Fr AE was in his forties. He enjoyed good health and felt affirmed in his parish priestly ministry every time he succeeded in getting something off his 'To Do List'. In the main he found that involving others delayed outcomes and consequently he dropped working with a Pastoral Council a number of years ago. Two years ago he received a request from his bishop to replace Fr Finbarr who was retiring as PP in St Clare's parish. Fr Finbarr was concerned that he would be the last resident priest in St Clare's and had spent much time and energy actively encouraging lay people to be very engaged in all aspects of parish life. They resisted initially, unsure as to what he wanted from them, but for the past four years more than forty lay people were actively engaged in parish life on an ongoing basis.

If you have experienced being sidelined or brushed aside then you will more easily identify with Fr Finbarr's disappointment and the disappointment of a number of lay people in St Clare's. The now retired chairperson of the Pastoral Council is quite open about what she perceives as a major regression. Not happy to be part of a token Parish Pastoral Council she resigned, but privately, as she had no desire to offend 'the young priest or bishop'. No one is disappointed with Fr AE's personal contribution but a raft of goodwill, energy and expertise that was contributing to the building up of the parish has been displaced.

Were the bishop to ask Fr AE to go to a different parish next year, he will certainly have 'achievements' associated with St Clare's. Sadly, however, I fear he will be more remembered for failing to recognise and honour the potential and goodwill nurtured by his predecessor. In short much comes back to core values and consequent priorities. ❧

Another scenario:

❧ Fiona has been a member of her PPC for seven years. For the second and third years of these she served as secretary and for the past four she has served as chairperson. Her approach is greatly influenced by her occupation. She is in management and accustomed to researching possibilities, framing initiatives, delegating, seeking updates and communicating outcomes to others after meetings. It's second nature to her. Her PP, Fr Xavier, and other members of the Pastoral Council, recognising her strengths have 'let her at it' and up to last year were very pleased to be associated with her successes. The reality, however, is that over four years, the nature of their council has completely changed and what's more … no one wants to become the next chairperson! Each member has come to the conclusion that as they can't do the role in the way that Fiona does, it's best to leave it to new blood. On paper, in terms of accomplishments, it has been the most successful council ever, but 85 per cent of members have indicated that they do not wish to serve for another term! ❧

Is Fiona at fault? Is her parish priest? Of course not! What we have here is a great learning opportunity, one that gets straight to the matter of core values. There has been a push within our dioceses to establish a Pastoral Council in every parish, and at times this has been motivated by a concern that some parishes will not have a resident priest going forward. Will these parishes need people to manage Church affairs? Of course – but perhaps the more imminent questions are:

1. What young adults and children, given the participatory culture of our times, will see themselves as parishioners?
2. How is this dimension of identity to be modelled and nurtured within Pastoral Councils and parishes?

My most challenging work encounters, in terms of attaining positive and sustainable outcomes, are also the ones that can go either way. Without exception they have been with people training to serve on Parish Pastoral Councils. In most instances the challenge can be linked to a single word: 'consideration'. We all like the security of knowing we are in the right place and that we can contribute. When 50 per cent or more of a group joyfully embrace the vision underpinning a PPC's existence, training sessions tend to be life-giving. When this is not the case, and often for very legitimate reasons, I tend to depart with a three-fold disappointment: for the group, particularly the priest(s), and for the wider parish community. There are always reasons behind a person's willingness or unwillingness to serve and the degree of their commitment if willing. With regard to Parish Pastoral Councils much depends on the group's interaction and whether meaningful and sustainable workable arrangements are fostered and appreciated.

Gifted people like Fiona have a huge contribution to make but it's vital that their contribution incorporate the mentoring of others. More than ever Pastoral Councils, clergy and lay members, need to be encouraging a sense of team that extends into each parish. When a monastic community reached a certain size St Benedict perceived the need for others to join the abbot in exercising leadership.[16] This is equally true of parishes. Council officers and councils as a whole need to ask 'What are we doing that is empowering of one another and others regarding the mission of the Church in our parish?' We also do well too to approach such questions in the light of some advice St Benedict gave his abbots: 'Arrange everything that the strong have something to yearn for and the weak nothing to run from.'[17] Our answers may vary, partly influenced by the uniqueness of our parishes, but also by the vision held by each Pastoral Council. If councils are to be instrumental and influential then we must consider how potential is nurtured. It may involve taking the time to talk with one another and others in our communities in a deeper way. There are pockets of people in every community who desire to be heard, understood and supported in bearing their burdens. On occasion they form self-help groups, such as local cancer patient support groups. Sometimes they enjoy a link with parishes. Often times they don't. Pastoral Councils, oriented toward the care and well-being of all parishioners, do well to establish a link and to convey their support and solidarity. This too is exercising servant leadership and creating possibilities for Holy Spirit given charisms to find expression.

My own experience of this is that it takes time and that this transition is frequently accompanied by robust discussion, even to the point of striking an outsider as argumentative. Every time a group breaks new ground for itself, the internal cohesion and commitment of a council can experience a certain flux. For those of us who find the contradiction of an opinion we hold challenging, there can be a call not to take another's contribution personally or to get lost in our new felt emotion. Equally we can be challenged to speak up, particularly when a view expressed does not tally with our experience. All of this is profoundly healthy, a great sign of our maturation in faith. We see many instances in the New Testament where life improved for some person or group because of a healthy dispute.[18] As servants of Christ and the Church community we must explore all fears impacting on our thoughts and feelings, mindful that perfect love casts out fear (1 Jn 4:18).

Another pastoral leadership consideration can be the avoidance of certain topics and areas of ministry because the leaders in the group feel the need to contain discussion so as to avoid saying no to those who seek some assistance. Such engineering, whilst well motivated, finds a more interpersonal resonance in the Rule of St Benedict in his advice to the cellarer of each monastery (the monk charged with dispensing the goods of the monastery). Benedict emphasises that where it is necessary for the cellarer to say no it should be done with kindness in a sober and sensible manner, such that his 'no' does not come across as arbitrariness or a lack of concern.[19] This is characteristic of all great pastoral leaders and leadership groups. Equally a driving instructor, when teaching an adult to drive, has to be moderate, circumspect and reflective, identifying times when it is appropriate to intervene and times when it is best to remain silent. In this way she or he helps build the confidence of the learner. The same is true for the Pastoral Council. There are times when the prudent course of action is to lead from the front, and other times when it is best to take a step back. For example, initiatives pertaining to youth faith development tend to be more successful when young people have both a role in shaping them and evaluating their outcomes for themselves.

Encouraging them and others to foster this kind of diagnostic ability and to be leaders in their own right and spheres, can, when properly supported, contribute greatly to others' motivation and confidence. Such a gentle and encouraging leading of souls also allows Pastoral Council members opportunities to accompany from a distance rather than lead or manage, equally respecting the limited time they can give to this ministry.

A final story illuminating how St Benedict's insights may apply to realities known to struggling Parish Pastoral Councils:

> ❧ Over a twelve year period a parish in a neighbouring diocese had three changes of parish priest, each of whom I knew. I happened to meet a retired primary school principal from the parish at a social gathering and knowing his gift for reading his community I queried how the diversity had impacted on the parish. I was quite taken by his response. Fr A had initiated a church refurbishment programme and they were very pleased with the outcomes; Fr B had deepened their appreciation of the Eucharist and understanding of prayer, and Fr C was now supporting them to explore how best to live a Eucharistic Spirituality. I was reminded of God's benevolence. Though these men were very different in terms of personality, it was clear that God's work, as exercised by them, was characterised by a very meaningful continuity. ❧

Through my work I have grown to appreciate the priestly ministry more fully and the value parishes place in having a resident priest. I also know first-hand the tremendous love many priests develop for the communities they serve. Many are rightly esteemed as valued pastoral and spiritual leaders. All do their best and like the rest of us contend with the shadow side of human nature. For years, in Ireland at least, their appointment has been a clerical matter, overseen by the bishop. That approach has strengths and weaknesses. So long as it remains our norm, and there is no prior consultation with Parish Pastoral Councils or parish communities regarding faith related priorities and aspirations, the need for the community itself to foster processes of discernment and follow-through will be important.

Parishes dependent on clerical leadership cannot thrive and may not even survive. Ultimately priests come and go. Whilst some believe themselves called to build up the communities of faith they serve, others do not and reserve their energies to serving the practising members of these communities. Like lay people, clergy have different visions of parish, of ministry and of what is meant by co-responsibility. That a climate of courtesy pervades discussions between clergy and laity is important, but may not go far enough. The underpinning issue – Where does authority reside regarding the mission of Christ in our parishes? – is critical. While the Rule of St Benedict does not speak directly to parish life, an application of the values it espouses is possible. At the level of leadership, much that underpins the roles of abbot, dean, prior, cellarer and guest-master have relevance to parish clergy and Parish Pastoral Councils. We do well to explore it, principally by way of determining our own place in the mission of the Church.

In our Catholic tradition parish priests are perceived as holding the place of Christ in the community. They do not replace Christ for us, rather each one represents him, especially when exercising his sacramental ministry. We see his authority, so long as it does not become authoritarian,[20] as a great service to life and, as members of the lay faithful, tend to be at ease with his presidency of various parish events, liturgical and social. If we see in him someone going the extra mile for the sake of Christ, his Kingdom and our community, then, as committed Catholics we are also likely to entrust him with our spiritual and pastoral concerns. Just as we read our priest, he also reads us. He values our fraternal expressions of care just as we value his expressions of fraternal, paternal and maternal care for ourselves and our children.

As with others we like, when we receive a hearing from our priest, we appreciate our priest's need for this to be reciprocated. We appreciate he can experience the loneliness that accompanies certain elements of leadership and are more at ease with him once we have established a good working relationship. We also appreciate being animated by his preaching, in word and example, but when it comes to the credibility of his authority and his perception of the credibility of our authority, we hold one another to the same standard.[21]

I write this knowing that all Parish Pastoral Councils are a work in progress. It is early days but our challenge, taking a Benedictine perspective, is to strive for them to be fruitful days. While 'Parish Councils' oriented toward 'maintenance concerns' like fixing a leaking roof have been a feature of parish life in a significant number of parishes for about fifty years, 'mission oriented' PPCs are a relatively new phenomenon. A critical question, however, is whether the Holy Spirit is the wind behind their sails? If our answer is yes, then they are a pathway of discipleship in our time and in our communities.

Our perception of another's leadership and authority always has a bearing on our relationship with them. This is particularly the case when people work together. Sustaining fruitful and workable arrangements during times of major transition in parish life necessitates dialogue. Very strikingly, the democratic ways of thinking in society at large today have similarities in the Rule of St Benedict.[22] Benedict never sought functional obedience from his monks as an army general might seek from a soldier. In my experience clergy do not want that either. Rather they, like Benedict, seek the companionship of those with a sincere obedience of faith, people seeking their way to God, sometimes having previously rejected him.[23]

Like the monks of Benedict's time, today's committed Christians are aware of their weaknesses and sinful inclinations. We value efforts from within our parishes to encourage and support us to live out the gospel as best we can. Well-prepared liturgical events, particularly at Christmas and Easter, renew our faith and our hope. Our presence at these events, increasingly, is symptomatic of our spiritual hunger as distinct from our church identity. Increasingly, we (committed Catholics) recognise our need of fellowship and safe people, as distinct from places, with whom to explore our faith. Conversations, the kind that allows us to be real regarding our lives, tend to follow rather than precede experiences of authentic fellowship.[24] And all the time the progression must take cognisance of our other responsibilities such as parenting or managing a challenging job. Significantly the majority of us have no truck with the characterisation of the contemporary Christian as a near martyr in a harsh secular culture that has turned from God. It saddens us that so many have left us.[25] In some cases we don't have the headspace, inclination or will to respond. To my mind, that is of greater concern. Increasingly we know enough to know we don't know everything there is to know. God, more so than Church, remains a mystery, thankfully drawing us to himself … and for that we are joyful and grateful.

I began this chapter with a reference to my frequent contact with women and men of deep and abiding faith who serve on Parish Pastoral Councils. Many are part of the humble multitude that proclaims Church in action every single day in a myriad of ways. I encounter in them the spirituality of service spoken of by Jesus when he said, 'No; anyone who wants to become great among you must be your servant, and anyone who wants to be first among you must be your slave, just as the Son of Man came not to be served but to serve, and to give his life as a ransom for many' (Mt 20:26–28). I also know them as women and men conscious of their own frailty and appreciative that Christ, in his goodness, 'never crushes the bruised reed' (Is 42:3). Some, like myself, have experienced the Lord's correction[26] and in the process learned God's great desire to see us all formed in genuine love. Such salutary experiences are great gifts, helping us beyond the ideological and other prisons of our own creation. Such pruning of our faults[27] not only corrects us but also sets us up for mission. Perhaps this is why I find myself asking, particularly now, if the Lord is also seeking our cooperation in drawing our brothers and sisters into the light of salvation[28] through our service with Parish Pastoral Councils? In our humility we may think this unlikely, but what then are we to make of biblical texts that invite us to see ourselves as his missionaries and ambassadors?[29]

Such a noble enterprise is wholeheartedly dependent upon the goodwill of the Holy Spirit, but if it is God's desire to see Pastoral Councils evolve to being missionary, should we refuse? As free people we have a choice. What is it to be? Equally for those with a charism for leadership, perhaps the time has come to consider how we place it at his service, reorienting our personal spiritualities accordingly? Who we are to ourselves and how we see others do not stand in isolation. They have a significant bearing on our sense of his Church, and in particular our part in it. On our own we are not unlike a strand of cord woven into a strong rope, yielding strength in our togetherness for Christ. The fact that we are wounded in some way does not discount us. In fact it may even explain God's choice of us. If we have grown through reconciliation, bereavement and loss then our empathy or brokenness may well become a lifeline to God for others. At any rate it is both an exciting and daunting time. May the wisdom of all Holy Spirit inspired spirituality traditions, including the Benedictine, support us in saying, 'Yes Lord, I come to do your will'[30] and 'What is not possible to us by nature, let us ask the Lord to supply by the help of his grace'.[31]

Coming of Age

Notes

1 Irish Catholic Bishops' Conference, *Living Communion: Vision and Practice for Parish Pastoral Councils Today*, Dublin: Veritas, 2011, p. 12.

2 Irish Catholic Bishops' Conference, *Share the Good News: National Directory for Catechesis in Ireland*, Dublin: Veritas, 2010, pp. 189 ff.

3 Ibid., p. 190.

4 For more information, visit: www.alpha.org

5 Wil Derkse, *The Rule of Benedict for Beginners*, Collegeville: Liturgical Press, 2003, p. 66.

6 Like its cognates in other European languages – for example, *-skapr* (Old Norse), *-skab* (Danish), *-schap* (Dutch) and *-schaft* (German) – it also carries associations with verbs such as 'to create', 'to ordain' and 'to appoint'.

7 RB, Prologue, 8:13, 2:33–36; quoting Mt 6:33.

8 cf. Rm 2:7; Heb 11:13–16; 1 Pt 1:6–8, 16–21.

9 RB 2:7, 12, 17, 24–25.

10 RB 21, 64, 65, 66.

11 RB 31:13.

12 The framing of the chairperson's role cannot, according to Gospel values, be reduced to a servile model of leadership. That risks the parish being 'the priest's parish' and the baptised his minions. Increasingly we need to evolve our structures so that co-responsibility is both visible and real. It is the task of all called to leadership, ordained, religious and lay faithful, to raise the eyeline of each council regarding such matters. A passive laity or dominant clergy is not in keeping with the spirit of the Gospel.

13 Norvene Vest, *Friend of the Soul: A Benedictine Spirituality of Work*, Plymouth: Cowley Publications, 1997, pp. 102 ff.

14 Maria Boulding, 'Obedience' in Holdaway, *The Oblate Life*, pp. 168 ff.; Derkse, *The Rule of Benedict for Beginners*, pp. 25–27.

15 cf. Phil 2:12–13.

16 RB 21, 65, 66.

17 RB 64:19, cf. Gn 33:13 and RB 34.

18 For example, Acts 6:1–7, 15:13–29.

19 RB 31:13–16.

20 According to Dom Bernardo Olivera, Abbot General of the Cistercians of the Strict Observance from 1990 to 2008 and a recognised expert on how grace meets us in our humanity, authoritarianism is the first sign of authority in crisis. Another is failure on the part of key bodies and personnel to exercise authority, thereby furthering uncertainty. If we need to make our authority felt, then it is likely that we are making another's obedience resentful. If we fail to exercise legitimate authority, then we may be contributing to the corrosion of the faith. If we are wise, Olivera suggests, our authority will never result in silencing others but rather in making them think. It will also be sufficiently humble to acknowledge that we do not have all the answers. See: Dom Bernardo Olivera, 'The Service of Authority', *Alliance for International Monasticism (AIM) English Language Bulletin*, 2005, 84, 'The Art of Leadership', pp. 17–24.

21 This sentence also draws on poignant insights of Dom Bernardo Olivera, who noted that 'authority', though received from above, is underwritten from below

by the quality of each person's service. In his paper 'The Service of Authority', he suggested to fellow abbots that their credibility (and I suggest ours and others in parish ministry) is dependent on five things: 1) Our capacity to listen; 2) Our contact with the reality of others; 3) The coherence between our words and our deeds; 4) Our centring on the essential and important; 5) Our promptness in taking charge of situations within our competence. His paper also identifies four 'plagues of monastic authority', which we would also be wise to ponder: 1) The paternalism that abuses authority by confusing it with power; 2) The fraternalism that denies the diversity and hierarchy of services; 3) The maternalism that needs to protect and shelter; 4) The infantilism of the person who depends on others for gratification and assurance.

22 RB 3, 72.
23 cf. RB, Prologue, 2–3.
24 cf. RB 72:4–8.
25 Recent decades have seen a significant exodus of Catholics under fifty years of age from regular participation in the Sunday Eucharist. Many remain 'nominal Catholics' but clearly do not see our Church as a sanctuary, school of life or community of belonging. We can no longer be reticence at pastoral council level around acknowledging this development and its vast implications. It is presenting very significant questions and the best responses, to be authentic, will need to be local and experiential.
26 cf. 2 Sm 12.
27 cf. RB 64:12–15.
28 cf. Is 9:2; 1 Pt 2:9; Eph 5:14; Col 1:12.
29 cf. 1 Chr 16:23–24; Rm 10:13–14; Gal 6:6–10.
30 cf. Ps 40:6–8.
31 RB, Prologue, 41.

Chapter Seven

Evolving Parish Pastoral Initiatives: Humility as a Core Principle of Evangelical Catholicism

Come to me, all you who labour and are overburdened, and I will give you rest. Shoulder my yoke and learn from me, for I am gentle and humble in heart, and you will find rest for your souls. Yes, my yoke is easy and my burden light.

(Mt 11:28–30)

Now, therefore, after ascending all these steps of humility, the monk will quickly arrive at that perfect love of God which casts out fear (1 John 4:18). Through this love, all that he once performed with dread, he will now begin to observe without effort, as though naturally, from habit, no longer out of fear of hell, but out of love for Christ, good habit and delight in virtue. All this the Lord will by the Holy Spirit graciously manifest in his workman now cleansed of vices and sins.

(RB 7:67–70)

This chapter, like chapter six, aspires to support Parish Pastoral Council members to consider the service they currently offer and could offer going forward. Members experienced in leadership or management will know the importance of responding to felt needs. Members who have known a pastoral need that went unattended – for instance, not being welcomed into a parish community – will know the importance in another way. Whatever our experience we need to be mindful that not everyone sees the world and more specifically the parish and Catholicism as we do. It's for this reason that we begin with a brief exploration of what 'humility' is and then look to the words and phrase 'parish' and 'Evangelical Catholicism' respectively.

When I was growing up 'humility' was presented to me as a virtue. Today there are good people who associate it with an abjuration of holistic human development. For them it carries negative overtones. Some parents and teachers, for example, are reluctant to propose humility as a virtue or evangelical principle. They deem it inappropriate, at least until such time as a young person's ego has properly matured.[1] Those of us who know women and men who have emerged from their formative years excessively introspective and lacking in self-esteem may agree. It is very important that children learn assertiveness and master the social and other skills by which we boost a wholesome self-worth. Catholic and other Christian educators committed to the holistic development of children are very conscious of that. This commitment can be an expression of their partnering of Christ who continues to say to us, his disciples, 'I have come that you may have life and have it to the full' (Jn 10:10).

We must not, however, confuse developments that culminate in a lack of self-esteem with 'humility'. It is not to be confused with 'humiliation', something reprehensible. Humility derives from the Latin *humus*, meaning 'earth'. Christian Spiritualities point to a connectedness with the earth and, by extension, with all that inhabits our earthly sphere. At a spiritual level, it can be a quality we recognise and admire in other people, particularly people who have never forgotten their roots. Within Christian tradition we look to Christ and his encounters to get a vision of what truly humble people look like. Often we are led to an appreciation of associated qualities. For example Jesus' encounter with the 'good' thief on the cross speaks of the importance of honest self-appraisal and genuine self-acceptance (Lk 23:42–47). In Christ we have someone who was never opposed to people being justly assertive and someone who upheld the dignity of everyone he encountered. For those of us who find conflict very difficult, there is the temptation not to speak out the truth. This is not humility but rather cowardice.[2] When Jesus spoke, for example to the scribes and Pharisees, his words got him into trouble. It didn't stop him. He remained true. He remained humble.

Regarding 'parish' I would like to begin with a brief story:

> ❧ As Fr Matthew and the parish secretary were going through the notices that had been submitted for inclusion in the parish newsletter one struck them quite forcibly. It was from the secretary of the local GAA club requesting that parishioners be informed that from now on training for the under twelve's football team would take place on Sunday mornings at 11 a.m., , the same time as the parish's celebration of the Eucharist. The secretary and club officials, predominantly Catholic, perceived attendance at Mass as a weekly obligation to be fulfilled and foresaw no difficulties in so far 'as people can get Mass elsewhere'. The parish priest, on the other hand, was keen that parishioners would be supported to commit 'to their own parish Mass'. ❧

Thirty-five years ago, a Tuam priest and theologian, Enda Lyons, published a wonderful book *Partnership in Parish: A Vision for Parish Life, Mission and Ministry*. In the opening pages Enda drew attention to the two overlapping senses of 'parish' prevalent at that time. The first was that of the local unit of the organisation then and still spoken of as 'the Church', and the second, that of a people forming a local Christian community. After some deliberation Enda delivered the following insightful sentence:

> Despite its complex and complicated appearance, its many structures, the Church is, in one sense, something very simple. Basically it is people – people who are enriched by their experience of Jesus of Nazareth, who associate with

others who have the same experience and interest, and who avail of all the means which help them to follow him.[3]

The true identity and nature of our parishes cannot be communicated without direct reference to the person and mission of Jesus Christ. Ultimately every parish has its origin in his ministry. The inspiration for their instigation can be traced back to him. As organisational units of 'his' Church they continue to have a very important mission, one for which every member has been gifted by the Holy Spirit. St Paul reminds us that this giftedness is for the benefit of the wider community (1 Cor 12:4). In reality those of us who seek to live this truth are both gifted by the Holy Spirit and flawed or wounded owing to the prevalence of sin in our world. Consequently we need God and one another, and benefit when others – in their humility – recognise, appreciate and engage with life mindful that we are all human. Should we come into a parish pastoral leadership or service role, it is necessary that we see beyond ourselves to others, but always according to the mind of Christ. We are particularly fortunate when we and others recognise in him the basis of our unity, and can allow him be the matrix of our continued spiritual growth. Our service, ideally, is rendered to him and to his desire that we all enjoy fullness of life.

At the time Enda Lyons was writing, 'Christian community' was an attractive ideal, but then as now, quite challenging to foster. While individualism was not as rife in the 1980s as it is today, there were other challenges to cohesiveness including economic pressures, limited training for lay pastoral leadership roles, new life influences via television, limited understanding of the lay vocation and unhelpful mixed messaging; for example, some priests forming Parish Councils and others terminating them. At that time it was the custom of the majority of parishioners to come together to celebrate the Eucharist every Sunday. The Sunday Mass was then better understood as God's weekly gathering of his family within the confines of the parish.

We owe a great debt of gratitude to Fr Enda and others, including the priests who served in our parishes through the 1980s, 1990s and 2000s and who worked hard to deepen our understanding. Their provision frequently invited us, as parishioners, to see how in the early Church a different relationship existed between clergy and laity. Many of them were eager to see us outgrow false understandings of ourselves, especially views that identified us as subordinates of clergy or religious,[4] and that has fed the culture of passivity that is rampant in some parishes. And yet, though we have been told many times that by virtue of our baptism we too have been chosen and set apart, we can struggle to take this to heart. There is still a widespread tendency to see the Church as the domain of the clergy and for the majority of lay people not to exercise any part in its internal and external affairs.[5] It's another reason why Parish Pastoral Councils are vital. In a spirit of humble service they can do much to support the renovation of parishes as communities of followers of Jesus Christ – frequently winning people over through small but meaningful initiatives.

This brings me to 'Evangelical Catholicism'. I first came upon it as a title of a book by George Weigel, a Catholic conservative American author, political analyst and social activist.[6] Weigel is steeped in our Catholic faith and this particular book has been recommended by many senior and influential Church figures, such as: Timothy Cardinal Dolan, Archbishop of New York; Carl A. Anderson, Supreme Knight of the Knights of St Columbus; Charles J. Chaput OFM, recently retired Archbishop of Philadelphia; Mary Ann Glendon, Learned Hand Professor of Law at Harvard Law School and a former United States Ambassador to the Holy See; Mary Eberstadt, a highly regarded America essayist and writer; and Philip Tartaglia, Archbishop of Glasgow. One of Weigel's assertions, widely held and accepted, is that a deep reform of the Catholic Church has in fact been underway for more than one and a quarter centuries.

It began with Pope Leo XIII. It continued in one way through the revitalisation of Catholic biblical, liturgical, historical, philosophical and theological studies in the mid-twentieth century. It continued in another, and at least as important, way in the martyrdom of millions of Catholics at the hands of the mid-twentieth century totalitarian systems. It was furthered by Pope Pius XII in his teaching on the Church 'as the mystical body of Christ'. It reached a high-water mark of ecclesiastical drama in the Second Vatican Council. It was given new impetus by Pope Paul VI in the 1975 apostolic letter *Evangelii Nuntiandi*, which called the entire Church to a new sense of missionary fervour in proclaiming the Gospel. And it has been brought into sharper focus by the pontificates of two men of genius, Blessed John Paul II and Benedict XVI. Many of Catholicism's twenty-first century struggles – for example, the sexual abuse crisis and the radical secularisation of Europe – reflect the churning of these deeper currents of reform, the resistance they have encountered, and the slow difficult emergence of a new way of being Catholic: a new 'form' of Catholicism. This new form is essentially continuity with Catholicism's origins and doctrinal development, for otherwise it would not be a genuinely Catholic 'form' of being the Church. But it is also something new. Perhaps better, it is the rediscovery and redeployment, in twenty-first century guise, of something quite old, something that goes back to the first centuries of the Christian era. It is called here, Evangelical Catholicism.

... EVANGELICAL CATHOLICISM IS THE CATHOLICISM THAT IS BEING BORN, OFTEN with great difficulty, through the work of the Holy Spirit in prompting deep Catholic reform – a reform that meets the

challenges posed to Christian orthodoxy and Christian life by
the riptides of change that have reshaped world culture since
the nineteenth century.[7]

It is a concept, encapsulating an invitation in sacred scripture,
in our living tradition to live out our Christian identity and not
to be fearful of engaging in conversations, consultations and
dialogues that facilitate us to name our experience, our need and
our aspirations as twenty-first century disciples of Jesus Christ.

Here is an example of 'Evangelical Catholicism' in action:

&❧ Eleanor and Eileen are good friends of many years and meet
monthly for coffee and a chat. Retired from work they both help
out with their grandchildren. They are very conscious of the
pressures on their children – mortgages, work commitments,
homework, ferrying the children to and from extracurricular
activities. They are careful to maintain a good working
relationship with their daughter-in-laws and for this reason they
are reserved around speaking about certain topics. Both have
a desire to see their grandchildren grow in the faith and are
disappointed that the culture isn't in their favour.

Eleanor's parish runs a pre-sacramental programme for
parents over four nights and she babysits on the evenings it runs.
Though they are tired, her son and daughter-in-law go. Initially
they went out of loyalty to her. They know she is disappointed
that they do not bring the children to Mass at weekends and so it
seemed a good way of communicating 'we're still interested and
we don't want religion coming between us'. They have also been
taken by the faith of some of their children's friends' parents. It
came as a surprise that some of them prayed with their children
every night before bedtime.

Eileen's parish doesn't have any pre-sacramental programme
and from chats with her grandchildren she's not getting the

impression that First Communion and Confirmation are being greeted as significant religious moments. Her parish priest, in her eyes, 'is not the kind of priest you can talk to about this stuff'. She feels powerless and constantly tells Eleanor how lucky Eleanor is in having parish support. Neither women are aware that there is a Parish Pastoral Council in their parish and Eleanor doesn't know that it was the council that were instrumental in getting the pre-sacramental programme established. ❧

Through my work I have come to appreciate every parish's uniqueness, particularly as a network of Christian faith communities. I have also observed that those that are growing are fortunate in having individuals, clergy, religious and laity, who foster a culture of mutuality. What do I mean by this? True Christian community, in my experience, is always contingent on the self-denial of at least some members. Without people open to serving others and committed to struggling against the lazy inertia that militates against true generosity of spirit, modern day parishes, especially rural parishes, are vulnerable to rapid decline. The humility of those who put the parish before self-interest frequently paves the way for others to experience parish as a Christian faith community. This can be expressed in a variety of ways – liturgical (lay participation in the preparation and execution of liturgies), pastoral care (outreach to older parishioners), fostering belonging (organisation of parish celebrations that bring people together), formative (outreach to parents and young people) and spiritual (finding expression in a variety of prayer initiatives like Advent and Lenten scripture based prayer groups).

Eleanor's parish, at the level of faith community, is much more alive than Eileen's. At this stage the networks that have developed energise her parish priest. It is five years since they introduced the pre-sacramental programme for parents. It took a lot of work, mostly communications work as parents were asking, 'Why have we to do this?' The perseverance of the parish priest and others has paid off. As a priest it has afforded him opportunities to get to know the parents and grandparents who were interested in raising their children in the faith. He had contact before but it was more superficial. More recent years have also been much easier. Why? Because some of the parents remain on as leaders for the coming year. Another spin off has been the rejuvenation of the altar-serving ministry among children and the willingness of some parents to become Ministers of the Word. Some parents, experiencing his care of them and their children through the programme, have also availed of opportunities to confide in him. He is also better positioned to support, discretely and confidentially, those struggling with relationship difficulties. There is a growing sense of being the one community of faith, each playing their part.

I began this chapter with Jesus' teaching in Matthew 11:28–30: 'Come to me, all you who labour … and learn from me, for I am gentle and humble in heart … Yes, my yoke is easy and my burden light.' I also noted earlier in this chapter that the Benedictine family, like many other Christian spiritual families, look to Jesus as the supreme example of a humble person. His earthly life, however, unlike ours, was uncomplicated by sin. His capacity to listen attentively to the voice of the Father and of the Spirit contributed greatly to his capacity to be humble. Building on this realisation Dom Michael Casey notes that 'Humility is that network of attitudes that springs from a radical conversion of heart, and signals a deep inner conformity with Christ'. Its growth in us can be powered by 'the simple desire to become like Christ'.[8] Considered in light of Eleanor and Eileen's experiences, his words, at first glance may seem irrelevant. However, let's consider them from another standpoint. Let's imagine that Christ is the instigator of the developments in Eleanor's parish and that the Holy Spirit has the good fortune of encountering people who are open to his inspiration and encouragement. For a family over an eighteen-month period to go from not participating in the Sunday Eucharist to a parent or parents participating in a four-session pre-sacramental programme, to their children becoming altar servers, to one of the parents becoming a Minister of the Word and to all conversing occasionally about their priest's homily is a radical turnabout. When that is also accompanied by a reintroduction or introduction of family prayer, then we can speak of a radical conversion taking place. Radical does not mean dramatic. And in the case of Eleanor's parish, it can all be traced back to the humility of a Pastoral Council acknowledging their parents need to be supported.

Herein lies an example of what 'Evangelical Catholicism' looks like and there are many other examples that could be communicated. For example, the deacon and his wife who opted to journey with three teenagers through a Youth Alpha programme. Today those young women are Eucharistic Ministers in their parish and every teenage boy and girl who comes to Mass in that parish now knows that 'Church ministries are not reserved to old people!'

One of my friends, Tommy, also recounts an experience that is illuminating from another angle:

> Tommy and his wife, Tanya, moved parish prior to the birth of their second child. When they enquired about baptism they were informed that it would be necessary to undertake a three-session baptism course. They responded by saying that wouldn't be necessary as it was their second child. The parish secretary smiled back at them and said, 'It will if you want your child baptised in this parish!' Two weeks later the two of them headed off with grumbling hearts to their first session. I rang next evening to see how they had gotten on and to encourage them to stay the course. Tommy surprised me. 'Justin, it was great. We met and got to talk with fourteen other couples in

the area. There were also five women and men from the parish, the priest, two parents and two grandparents who spoke of their experience of raising children. The priest, Fr Luke, won the respect of everyone in the room. He told us that choosing baptism was about choosing a community within the broader community and that we needed to be there for one another as well as for our children. He told us we had no business getting Tommy Junior baptised if we didn't get that! The parents and grandparents also spoke to us about minding ourselves and our relationships with our spouses, and it was nice how everyone was as respectful of couples that weren't married as those that were.'

When Tanya came on the phone she emphasised meeting the other mums and shared how she had got the number of a good babysitter. I got another glimpse of the success of the programme at the baptism when 'the baptism team' warmly welcomed us and stood in the porch with us as Fr Luke took Tommy Junior in his arms and lovingly proclaimed 'Tommy, the Church welcomes you with great joy!' Since that time Tommy, Tanya and their family like to go to Mass on the first Sunday after Christmas, the Feast of the Baptism of Our Lord. All those who have had a child baptised are invited to come to the 11 a.m. Mass that day and to linger for a time afterwards. Micky, an elderly Pastoral Council member in the parish, someone I know as a lovable elderly grouch and wit, has labelled it 'Raucous Sunday' as young children at the pre-discipline stage of life make their presence felt. In truth Micky doesn't mind. In fact he misses their presence the following Sunday when the worshipping community begins to resume its post-Christmas character. ❧

Should your motivation to serve on your Pastoral Council be waning, I hope you are finding some encouragement here. There are parishes that are growing, each sapling of new growth weathering the various storms that come its way, and there are parishes that are dying for want of collective leadership. Those that are transitioning into more vibrant pastoral communities have something in common. They are not seeking to fill their churches at the weekends. Rather they are devoting energy to recognising felt needs and response possibilities, and they are fostering these as best they can. In every instance there are four critical aspects:

1. Women and men, and not just a priest, self-giving in the service of others.
2. Having an exploratory forum to tease out felt needs, related issues and possibilities, such as a Parish Pastoral Council.
3. A commitment to widening ownership and involving others.
4. Good communication – letting people know the background and aspirations behind the development(s).

As alluded to earlier, it may also be time for parish communities, through their Parish Pastoral Councils, to pause momentarily in order to ask 'How are we?' God's callings, though unambiguous, can be challenging to decipher. Within our calling to holiness of life lies another, the calling to participate in the mission of the Church. It is good to note these are 'callings' as distinct from 'tasks', and frequently are best faced with others. Jesus, as we will recall, sent his disciples out in pairs. We also need the blessing, inspiration and graces that come with journeying with a friend. The Blessed Trinity will not be found wanting in bestowing us, through every Sunday Eucharist as well as through other means, with the graces we need. Living up to them will at times be characterised by struggle, both at the level of discerning what to do and then doing it. Psychologically we may need to outgrow some self-imposed restrictive ways of thinking. For example, those of us who find it quite challenging to participate in discussions concerning the planning and promotion of events and initiatives oriented toward our and others' spiritual growth, do well to ask ourselves why this is? The individualism permeating our culture is causing us to privatise our faith in a way Christ never intended. Equally we may need to examine absorbed attitudes and beliefs regarding our place in our parish community. To use an old axiom, are we just there to pray, pay and obey? These too are reasons why Pastoral Councils as consultative forums within parishes are vital.

In the prologue of his Rule, St Benedict speaks of the need to 'prepare our hearts and bodies for the battle under holy obedience (attentive listening)'[9] so as to attune ourselves to God and come into his service. As previous chapters attest, he leaves his hearer/reader with no illusions. Challenging issues, as well as periods of consolation, face all who seek to be attentive to Christ. Moments of fatigue, lassitude and duties we would prefer to be without are common to all who seek to contribute to the work of the Kingdom. Like Benedict's monks, we may find that an integral response requires that we undertake duties initially repugnant or unsettling to our sensitivities. Most times these are likely to be in the sphere of inconvenience until we establish systems to support us.[10] From time to time the forefront of 'the battle' of which St Benedict speaks can be our own inertia. Sometimes it is something much more challenging and so he reminds us that 'what is not possible for us by nature, let us ask the Lord to supply by the help of his grace'.[11] Rather than get upset or throw in the towel it is good to come before the Lord with a humble and contrite heart and to ask his assistance. Yes, we need to be humble with God, one another and ourselves!

My friend, Jack, testifies to the power of this. One story from his bank of stories about God's providence concerns an occasion when, having heard a missionary priest speak, he felt a calling to fundraise to help a parish in Africa establish a school. After praying about it he told some friends about his aspiration. Within a few weeks they and others had formed a committee and were up and running. He believes, and I am inclined to agree, that every time we seek to give ourselves to the heartfelt needs of others, we are giving ourselves to Christ. He also believes that Christ frequently helps us through the goodwill of others as he is active in their hearts and minds too. It can also be quite humbling to admit our need of help but I am forever taken by the eagerness of children in particular, to help when and where they can. No wonder Jesus invites us to follow their lead.[12]

According to Benedict spiritual maturation requires a conscious effort on our part to become more humble disciplined persons. Drawing inspiration from sacred scripture,[13] the writings of other saints and other monastic rules,[14] he calls on each of his monks to ascent in holiness through humility.[15] To support them (and now us) he presents the image of a twelve-rung ladder, a recurring image of spiritual progress inspired by Jacob's dream (Gn 28:12). He uses this ladder to symbolise twelve concrete steps that he recommends to all who seek to truly love God and neighbour. His rationale is also scripture based: 'For everyone who raises himself up will be humbled, and the one who humbles himself will be raised up' (Lk 14:11).

These twelve steps, re-crafted as directives, may be summarised as follows:

1. Hold to a reverent awareness of God's presence at all times,[16] seek to be attentive to God, and always put God's will before your own.
2. Join Christ in living John 6:38 as best you can: 'I have come not to do my own will, but the will of him who sent me.'
3. Submit to your superior in all obedience for the love of God, imitating Christ who was obedient, 'even unto death' (Phil 2:8).
4. When obedience proves difficult quietly embrace and endure related suffering without weakening or seeking escape.
5. Do not conceal from your superior any sinful thoughts entering your heart, or any wrongs committed in secret. Rather confess them humbly.

6. Be content with the lowest and most menial treatment, regarding yourself as an ordinary servant[17] in whatever task you are given.
7. Give up any illusions of superiority. You don't need to be better than the next person.[18]
8. Do only what is endorsed by the common rule of the community and the example set by your superiors.
9. Control your tongue and remain silent, not speaking unless asked a question.
10. Do not be given to ready laughter.
11. Speak gently and without laughter, seriously and with becoming modesty, briefly and reasonably, but without raising your voice.
12. Manifest humility in your bearing no less than in your heart.

Presented in this concentrated way, Benedict's teaching can initially appear austere and a vindication regarding reservations about the promotion of 'humility' recounted at the beginning of this chapter. His contextualisation, and references to humility in other parts of the Rule, however, demonstrate his primary goal to support us to grow in holiness. His teaching on humility is also the part of his Rule most laden with scriptural promises,[19] references and teachings.[20] Through these, Benedict seeks to grow both our resolve and understanding, and to encourage us. His ultimate goal is to help us give our hearts and minds to God, that the perfect love of God pervade us, casting out all fear.[21] Should we attain – through cooperation with God's grace – this level of sanctity, we shall, he says, be cleansed of all vices and sins, and by the power of the Holy Spirit, manifest God's glory.

Goals, when collectively and systematically pursued, carry greater possibility of realisation. There can be benefits too for those of us who put our shoulder to the wheel, as we continue to grow. We need to guard against pride. That is one of the reasons we do well to pray about our group commitments. Sanctity, for Benedict, is not primarily a matter of living an ethical code but of playing our part in fostering and living out of a conscious relationship with God. It is from this that we derive our energy, hope and liberation from all that weighs us down and those experiences that cause us hurt and frustration. It is not a matter of winning God's approval or being good enough to gain God's benevolence. Rather it is a matter of cherishing the God who is in and with us, the love of whom impels us to be cheerful and generous. Humility, in this sense, is a pathway to eternal life.[22]

Read in the light of the Rule in its entirety, and mindful that the Rule was directed to monks committed to community living, we more easily see that St Benedict's teaching on humility is principally oriented toward good relations. The moderate Benedict never focusses solely on inward states and dispositions. Such spiritualities, as Casey notes, 'isolate the individual from the Church's mission, and reduces the Kingdom of God to one's private struggles from probity and peace'.[23] A Pastoral Council comprising a membership either wholly disinterested in personal sanctity or preoccupied with their individual levels of sanctity has little to offer the wider Christian community.

Equally, the twelve steps proposed by Benedict point to a degree of humility, which like other evangelical principles, cannot be feigned. True humility does not lend itself to falsehood of any kind, particularly anything that is not genuinely liberating of the human spirit. A later disciple of Benedict's, St Bernard of Clairvaux, affirmed this when he highlighted that true humility is always grounded on truth: within oneself, in one's relations with others, and with regard to God.[24] This realisation sometimes accompanies a sense of discomfort with oneself for being less than true with others or annoyance owing to the inadequacy of another person's responses to our questions, particularly regarding matters of injustices, pastoral inaction, etc.

Again the implications for Pastoral Council members, and officers in particular, are highly significant. One of our key challenges is to generate a meeting culture that in its attentiveness to Christ, promotes truth across every conversation, even at the risk of offending sensibilities. There is an onus on all of us to be Christ-like, not only in our outreach to the marginalised but also in following Christ in expressing distaste, distrust and displeasure with views and proposals more burdensome than liberating of the human spirit.[25] Ultimately Benedict wants our expressions of humility to lead us to Christ in such a manner as we acknowledge him as our head, inspiration and goal.

Humility, according to Benedict, lies in knowing ourselves as children of the living God and in coming to know and accept what our lives are meant to produce. We succeed not through our attainment of perfection but by our humble perseverance. Through the twelve steps our eyes are opened to the Light that drives out the darkness[26] and to living a key phrase of The Lord's Prayer, i.e. 'thy will be done' (Mt 6:10). This, Benedict teaches, is quite challenging initially, particularly in our efforts to be vigilant against our most base desires.

Our first challenge may be to welcome God as God in our lives (step one) and to put God's will before our own. Step two is to pursue joint living with Christ who came to do the will of God the Father (Jn 6:38). At both the personal and communal levels we can often feel unsure about what this is. I continue to be inspired by an answer offered by Sr Joan Chittister OSB:

> The will of God for us is what remains of a situation after we try without stint and pray without ceasing to change it.[27]

The following advice of Basil Hume OSB has also helped me integrate what is meant here:

> If you know there are going to be moments ... when things
> will be difficult (e.g. work will be hard, boring, unrewarding),
> of times when you will suffer ... then accept them as crosses
> which you have to carry this day. Just say: 'Thy will be done,
> dear Lord, not mine. Let all these things bring me closer to
> Thee. That is how Our Lord prayed.' [28]

We are not meant to be living as if God does not exist or inferior
to us in love and understanding. To know, love and serve him
begins with being in relationship with him and being open to his
benevolence, not just to us but to everyone and all creation. In this
humility, this truth, this relationship, our lives can flower in ways
impossible, if we, in our freedom, choose differently.

Step three, submitting to one's superior (actively listening for
the wisdom of another for the love of God, imitating Christ who
was obedient, 'even unto death'), frees us from assuming that we
have the definite response or answer to a problem. It reminds us
that humility also lies in obedience (attentive listening) to the
words, directions and insights of those who are called to be a voice
of Christ in our lives. It reminds us to check that we are not acting,
unwittingly or otherwise, out of arrogance. It is a step that brings
many of us face to face with our struggle for autonomy, power and
authority beyond ourselves – for our own good as much as that of
others.

Step four (When obedience proves difficult quietly embrace
and endure related suffering) is another that can have a corrective
influence. To embrace suffering when obedience proves difficult
is ever a test of character, especially if we know ourselves to be in
the right and our superior in the wrong. According to the Rule it
is, nevertheless, more right that we be open to the word of God
through others, even to the point of having to accept such suffering.
How so? Because in the process we develop true perseverance
and learn to forgo being our own guides and watchdogs. It is

more right, according to Benedict, to grow from certain difficult situations than to reject them. One known fruit is a high level of emotional stability, secured through learning new levels of self-control by withstanding consequent internal storms over and above allowing ourselves to be tossed about or taking respite in a harbour of discontent.

When I first sought to apply step five (Not concealing from my superiors any sinful thoughts entering my heart, or any wrongs committed in secret) to group settings, I ran into difficulty. Here too I am indebted to Sr Joan Chittister OSB:

> The fifth rung of the ladder of humility is an unadorned and disarming one: self-revelation, Benedict says, is necessary for growth. Going through the motions of religion is simply not sufficient. No, the Benedictine heart, the spiritual heart, is a heart that has exposed itself and all its weaknesses and all its pain and all its struggles to the One who has the insight, the discernment, the care to call us out of our worst selves to the heights to which we aspire.
>
> The struggles we hide, psychologists tell us, are the struggles that consume us. Benedict's instruction, centuries before an entire body of research arose to confirm it, is that we must cease to wear our masks, stop pretending to be perfect, and accept the graces of growth that can come to us from the wise and gentle hearts of people of quality around us.
>
> Humility such as this gives us energy to face the world. Once we ourselves admit what we are, what other criticism can possibly demean us? Once we know who we are, all the delusions of grandeur, all the righteousness that's in us dies and we come to peace with the world.[29]

The invitation to be content (step six) with the lowest and most menial treatment, regarding oneself as 'a poor and worthless servant' in whatever task one is given, is also quite countercultural for us. A critical phrase here is 'be content'. There is a challenge for all of us in discovering we can be happy without receiving any special treatment. Ultimately this step invites us to learn to be self-emptying so that our souls will always have space to breathe, and be open to the graces of the situations in which we find ourselves. This counteracts all tendencies to think of fields being greener elsewhere and of hankering after remote, false or distant possibilities to the detriment of what is possible.

Step seven (Give up any illusions of superiority. You don't need to be better than the next person[30]) also centres on our liberation from false expectation. Those who are humble regarding their capacities and do not exalt themselves have no need to be untruthful. When we embrace our smallness we have little need to disguise, hide or lie about our frailties. We are also liberated to meet others in their frailty with gentleness and calm, particularly those whose frailty has come to light in an indecent or crude manner. Adoption of this step fosters our aptitude for kindness, sensitising us to our own and others' shortcomings.

At the level of group meetings and projects, steps six and seven can also receive expression in our efforts to be unthreatening around others, of meeting co-members with open hands and an attitude of receptivity. Earlier in the Rule, Benedict has highlighted the importance for everyone aspiring 'to know nothing more dear than Christ'.[31] For such an attitude to supersede our desire for human affirmation, humility must flower. Such receptivity to Christ is also represented in RB 53 with regard to responding to all our brothers and sisters in their need over and above any aspirations we may have for ourselves. This humble self-giving is the backbone of many of the fine pastoral initiatives currently giving expression to Evangelical Catholicism at parish level.

The invitation of step eight (Doing only what is endorsed by the common rule of the community and the example set by your superiors) encapsulates an invitation to be a team player. It also invites us to ponder the leadership styles of those charged with building up our faith communities. It invites us to stay within the stream of local life, accruing its wisdom and valuing the truths handed down to us. Here we are encouraged to attach ourselves to the holy and wise people in our midst, thus minimising the risk of becoming our own blind guides, and optimising their influence on our spiritual and human quest for fulfilment in this life and the next. The invitation is to live faith together and not to embark on spiritual solo runs that ultimately distance us from others.

Moderations in speech and laughter (steps nine, ten and eleven) require little explanation for those of us who, to use a colloquial expression, 'have put our foot in it'! I anticipate we would also agree that needless chatter and gossip dissipates energy and risks reputations. Equally these steps speak to those of us who have been disappointed with ourselves or others for using humour to prevent a discussion from receiving the weight and consideration it deserved. While the service of God through pastoral initiatives can contribute to ineffable joy, we do well to guard against vanity and vain-glory. Politeness and good manners must be more than a front. When they become the fruit of interior humility and charity, they radiate a grace that builds up community and serves other Gospel values. We imitate Christ more fully when we keep guard over our mouths and embody his beatitudes.[32]

These steps also contain a call to those of us of 'strong personality' to sensitise ourselves to the differing personality types of others. Depending on our personality we may need to exercise a personal discipline so as to allow others the scope they require to grow, mature and flourish. In this context I recall the personal sharing of a priest who found a change of parish very difficult, and who after a year, was considering asking his bishop for a new appointment:

❧ Within the parish there were a number of strong personalities among the lay faithful. They were, to quote him, 'the best in the world when it comes to helping out and fundraising but also very undermining'. Within a few weeks of his arrival he experienced a coordinated effort on their part to have him reinvigorate certain devotional practices, increase the number of Masses and commit parish funds to projects that had their approval but that had not been discussed within the parish at large. He felt a particular clerical mould was being imposed on him, to the point of identifying it as a personal mental health issue. He was also experiencing frustration as his efforts to encourage conversation via the Parish Pastoral Council had given rise to venting on the part of those who weren't getting their way. The net impact was that others, who he was encouraging to become involved, had declined his invitation. He was also finding it difficult to discuss his concerns with the women and men who wanted him to advance according to their vision and will. 'They don't appear to realise it, but they are treating this parish as their personal domain and treating the rest of us like minions. They don't appear to get "co-responsibility". It seems to be there way or no way.' ❧

The call to manifest humility in our bearing (step twelve) is one I associate with many older people who have given generously of themselves through a lifetime of Church and family ministry. In them humility has moved from the heart to the body and now exudes through a very hospitable disposition. What impresses me most is how they retain this demeanour, and how, in their company, I and others feel a fraternal spiritual bond.[33] Frequently they exude the grace of serenity. One senses that through their own trials and tribulations they have become 'friends of God',[34] daily placing their trust in him.

Individually and collectively all twelve steps oppose pride of any kind. Graciously engaging with and yielding to a superior, or

Parish Pastoral Council decision, with whom we don't fully agree, or undertaking menial tasks, whilst initially difficult, help us grow into spiritual maturity. Learning to value, honour and undertake the often obscure, laborious and sometimes monotonous occupations that accompany pastoral developments for others can also impact positively on our growth. Just as countless Benedictines over the past 1,500 years have been supported through the steps to inculcate an interior acceptance of the dying and rising characteristic of true spiritual growth, so too with us. We are more fully Christ's when we joyfully interiorise Jesus' powerful teaching: 'So, with you: when you have done all you have been told to do, say, "We are useless servants: we have done no more than our duty"' (Lk 17:10). My own experience of struggling to live this spirituality is that I am frequently reminded of two things: my need of God and the power of God's grace to help us (groups) attain our objectives. Our potentiality and capacity is limited. Only when we look to God in the spirit of the Gospel are there outcomes of note. Invariably the processes along the way require us to be humble, both in relation to our shortcomings and concerns. This is the reason this chapter bears the subtitle, 'Humility as a Core Principle of Evangelical Catholicism'.

    ❧ Many years ago a friend was asked to take a leadership role in a group. He declined on the grounds of inexperience. The outgoing leader spoke to him privately and offered to mentor him. Her gracious sensitivity was the push he needed. His reality and the group's was that they needed her in this capacity. Years later he happened to be in a leadership role in another group. A courageous member, to whom he will be forever indebted, challenged him privately concerning his leadership style. The question he was asked was simple but stinging, 'Did he realise that he was putting the group in jeopardy by holding too tight a reign during discussions?' He rang me, seeking someone with whom to process his thoughts and feelings. Over coffee he realised there was more than a grain of truth behind the question but he had not been conscious of it. Rather he became aware that a lot of his energy was taken up in a duty he had imposed upon himself, that of ensuring outcomes arising from their discussions did not generate tensions in other quarters. Unwittingly he had disrespected the integrity of the other members. Communication had become superficial. Had it gone unchecked, he would have seriously undermined commitment to the group and its mission. What was lacking in him, thankfully, was not lacking in the person who called him aside: the humility to ask the painful question for the greater good, in this instance at the risk of their budding friendship. Ultimately the whole experience proved liberating for him. It also taught us that one's superior is not always the person who holds an office but rather the one of greatest integrity, the one, as in this instance, who speaks the truth. ❧

Like others I greatly admire pastoral leadership styles that accommodate different viewpoints and dissenting voices in the pursuit of harmony and positive outcomes. Such leaders are often mindful too of the need to create space for the talents and abilities of others, even when it entails a personal loss on their part – a loss of the limelight, control and temporary peace of mind. I think particularly of a gracious choir director who invited a relatively new member to sing the prized post communion solo at the end of Christmas Midnight Mass and who was also first to congratulate her. Having been the singer herself this was amongst her most cherished experiences. The Christmas liturgy was enhanced for her parish community, but not without a personal cost. In her humility she did a lot for her friend.

Returning to Parish Pastoral Councils, I cannot think of any that I have sat with for more than an hour that were not characterised by divergent tendencies. In some instances the lines of demarcation fell between those who liked to be project-based and were drawn to practical initiatives, and those who tended to be more reflective and spiritually inclined. It was always very interesting when the demarcation presented around liturgical challenges. The value of such diversity manifested when the practically minded discerned mechanisms to capitalise on the reflected insights of the spiritually minded. In these and other instances a principle of complementarity became apparent. In my experience, where relationships are characterised by mutual respect and common awareness of need, diversity follows, with members more readily recognising how they can contribute. A final story:

> Recently an elderly woman in our parish developed a debilitating infirmity. Her husband, who enjoys good health, and other family members now support her in new ways. All their lives have adapted and no one in our community is surprised. This, after all, is what families do when a family member needs additional support.

Could the same ring true in parish life? Might the neediness of the weak and vulnerable, including those at the fledgling stages of faith development and church belonging, be met through the resourcefulness of the strong in faith? In family and working life many of us draw on our resourcefulness in unanticipated ways on an ongoing basis. Could it be that there are significant needs now presenting at parish level that merit a generous response but that there is something dysfunctional about our way of being Church that is preventing us from responding appropriately? Is the time yet right for us to review and humbly reconsider our pastoral priorities? I anticipate many, and particularly those with the ability to foresee the potential communication difficulties and misunderstandings will be reticent about going there. Every such enterprise places significant demands on a few. They too may be reticent. At any rate we remain extraordinarily privileged as women and men free to constantly draw upon the life and vitality of Christ our Risen Lord in the power of the Holy Spirit. In this and every moment he is the one to whom we should turn, the one who is *gentle and humble of heart,* and who alone can *grant rest to our souls* (Mt 11:29) and the souls of all those restless women and men who have yet to entrust themselves to him.

Notes

1   Those who feel the need to protect others always have due cause. It's important to evaluate whether their reactions and ours to 'humility' are a negative repercussion of a bygone era. I think particularly of a time when women and people of lower social strata were wrongly socialised to be accepting of an inequitable and unjust status quo, to 'humbly' accept their situation.

2   Columba McCann OSB, 'The School of The Lord's Service in the Gospel According to Matthew', an oral presentation to Benedictine Oblates of Glenstal Abbey, 1 August 2020.

3   Enda Lyons, *Partnership is Parish: A Vision for Parish Life, Mission and Ministry*, Dublin: Columba Press, 1986, p. 9.

4   This was taken up in chapter six.

5   Here I draw on a prophetic observation of Karl Rahner's. See Karl Rahner, *Theological Investigations*, Vol. 8, London: DLT, 1971, p. 7.

6   George Weigel, *Evangelical Catholicism: Deep Reform in the 21st-Century Church*, New York: Basic Books, 2015. Weigel is possibly better known in Ireland and the UK as a biographer of St Pope John Paul II *(Witness to Hope)* and as a Vatican analyst for NBC news.

7   Ibid., pp. 3–4.

8   Michael Casey, *A Guide to Living in the Truth: Saint Benedict's Teaching on Humility*, Missouri: Liguori Publications, 2001, p. 8.

9   RB, Prologue, 40.

10 For example, the Altar Server Coordinator who dislikes having to remind parents of new recruits of the Masses where there children are due to assist.

11 RB, Prologue, 40.

12 cf. Mt 18:3

13 cf. Lk 14:11, 18:14; Ps 130(131):1; Gn 28:12.

14 For example, Rule of St Basil.

15 See chapter seven of The Rule of St Benedict.

16 As recommended in Ps 35(36):2.

17 RB uses the phrase 'poor and worthless servant'.

18 In offering this synopsis, I am drawing on insights of Fr Columba McCann OSB in 'The School of The Lord's Service in the Gospel According to Matthew', an oral presentation to Benedictine Oblates of Glenstal Abbey, 1 August 2020.

19 cf. Mt 10:22; Rm 8:37; Ps 105(106):1; Ps 118(119):71, 73.

20 cf. Ps 7:10, 93(94):11, 138(139):3, 75(76):11, 17(18):24; Sir 18:30; Mt 6:10; Prov 16:26; Ps 37(38):10; Prov 15:3; Ps 13(14):2–3; Ps 49(50):21; Jn 6:38; Phil 2:8; Ps 26(27):14; Rm 8:36; Ps 65(66):10–12; 2 Cor 11:26; 1 Cor 4:12; Ps 31(32):5, 72(73):22–23.

21 RB 7:67–68; cf. 1 Jn 4:18.

22 RB 7:5.

23 Casey, *A Guide to Living in the Truth*, p. 7.

24 Further expounded in Casey, *A Guide to Living in the Truth*, pp. 17–28.

25 cf. Lk 9:37–56, 11:37–54, 20:45–47; Mt 23:1–39; Mk 12:35–40, 16:14.

26 RB 7:10–22.
27 Joan Chittister OSB, *The Rule of St Benedict: A Spirituality for the 21st Century*, New York: Crossroad, 2010, p. 84.
28 Basil Hume OSB, *To Be a Pilgrim: A Spiritual Notebook*, Slough: St Paul Publications, 1984, p. 111.
29 Ibid., p. 89.
30 Summarised earlier as 'Admit with your tongue and be convinced in your heart that you are inferior to all and of less value'.
31 RB 5:2.
32 cf. Mt 5:5–15.
33 St Augustine, perceiving something similar as hospitality, has written: 'O truly holy hospitality, the friend of angels, the sister of love, the crown of humility! Whoever possesses you possesses true humility! Whoever possesses humility, practises true hospitality. Brothers, let not only the Fathers teach us to keep hospitality holy, but let us also learn humility from Christ … This is the perfect foundation of hospitality. O truly holy humility, sister and graceful friend of hospitality. Whoever possesses you sees himself in everything as more insignificant than others. Never does he yearn to appear superior to others. He evades the first seats and detests all desire to dominate. Hospitality alone he embraces in love, hospitality alone he desires to practise.' Quoted from Eric Leland Saak, *Creating Augustine: Interpreting Augustine and Augustinianism in the Later Middle Ages*, Oxford: Oxford Scholarship Online, 2012.
34 cf. Gn 15:6; Jas 2:23.

Chapter Eight

Coming of Age:
Working Toward and Sustaining Partnership

With all humility and gentleness, and with patience, support each other in love. Take every care to preserve the unity of the Spirit by the peace that binds you together.

(Eph 4:2–3)

'Your way of acting should be different from the world's way; the love of Christ must come before all else.'

(RB 4:20–21)

One of the very striking elements of the Rule of St Benedict for twenty-first century readers is its treatment of people deemed guilty of serious faults. Eight chapters are devoted to punishment and its techniques, including exclusion from community life,[1] degrees of excommunication[2] (temporary exclusion from certain aspects of community life)[3], corporeal punishment[4] and the manner of reproving young people.[5] Not one of them, I anticipate, would be acceptable today. What is interesting from a Parish Pastoral Council perspective is what he deems punishable and his assertion that the need to punish was never an excuse for the arbitrary wielding of power, vengeance or anger.[6] For example, Benedict does not propose punishments for uncompleted tasks or lack of spiritual intensity or ignorance or weakness of the flesh. Rather his ire is raised regarding those who undermine the growth and cohesion of the community through their grumbling, defiance or apathy. In such cases he was also adamant concerning the need for atonement, especially when love, trust and cooperation – all necessary for a community to flourish – had been undermined. He advocates a culture in which we say, 'Enough, if you want to be a world unto yourself, then be one!' His reasoning, experts suggest, was that these 'exclusionary' forms of punishment would not crush the offending person but enable them to get their life in perspective and to start over with a new heart.

Joan Chittister OSB, while commenting on this aspect of the Rule, notes the value in everyone taking time to consciously explore if and what they are holding back from any group they have committed to.[7] She also perceives in Benedict's approach a need for people in leadership to put appropriate supports in place for everyone experiencing confusion, anger and depression. Those in leadership, she says, are not to model themselves on army drill sergeants or Olympic athlete coaches, but as doctors and shepherds tending the weak and carrying the lost. She notes:

> What we have in monasteries and parishes ... and most families are just people who never meet their own ideals and often, for want of confidence and the energy that continuing commitment takes, abandon them completely. Then, our role, the Rule of Benedict insists, is simply to soothe what hurts them, heal what weakens them, lift what burdens them and wait. The spiritual life is a process, not an event. It takes time and love and help and care. It takes our patient presence. Just like everything else.[8]

In St Benedict's eyes community enables us both to live the Christian life and to learn from it and it's a perspective worth pondering as we continue to explore the service Parish Pastoral Councils can render. Another is our personal take on our own vocation or calling.

In her book, *Friend of the Soul: A Benedictine Spirituality of Work*, Norvene Vest has written, 'Vocation is God's daily call to each of us to be what we are, i.e. human, and to allow our lives to unfold according to our intrinsic nature, to become what God knows us to be.'[9] There is an intimacy to this call which many of us value, grounded as it is in our personal relationship with God. Equally, there can be another dimension, one less appealing, a call not away from the world but toward it, into its messiness and disorder. This often requires some 'soul-work' on our part, sometimes taking years and generally necessitating that we embrace emerging difficulties with humility and trust (Jude 8:21–23). The unfolding of our souls in the service of God is never automatic. Rather it requires that we exercise our freedom in favour of God's healing graces. Thus we begin to disempower our prejudices and love our vulnerabilities out of existence. Many of us have deeply engrained defence mechanisms fearful of such a change in our way of being. They too need to be brought to consciousness and allowed to heal. Human by nature and design, we become saints through a series of choices grounded in love. The void in each of us that finds expression in superficial whims and appetites is symptomatic of something much more profound and beautiful. Our psyche, for all its genius, cannot fill its own emptiness. Only God can do that, and only if we let him!

And it's for these very reasons that we, as members of the faithful, are encouraged to nominate to Pastoral Councils not only women and men of known competencies, but also caring, compassionate individuals who seek to honour God in their day-to-day living. No one ever said the adventure of faith would be easy but we are greatly encouraged when women and men of proven character share the journey with us, offering support and encouragement.

The whole experience, however, points to an important consideration: our need of clarity, and when we don't have it, our need to acquire it. In committee, board and Pastoral Council work in particular, we tend to fare better when everyone is clear on the remit, the boundaries of our work and the proper ways of doing business. In my experience of working alongside Parish Pastoral Councils, I have found that those who have taken time to clarify expectations – their own and others – and where officers ensure that communication is not rushed, work best together and on occasion enjoy unanticipated outcomes.

A story to illuminate:

➥ Some years ago, two men of middle years accepted nominations to serve on their Parish Pastoral Council. At the time the idea of a link with a parish in the developing world was under consideration. Related communications with the other parish were quite frustrating for officers, primarily rooted in cross-cultural issues. When the discussions became known to parishioners via the Pastoral Council's report in the parish newsletter, some parishioners also became concerned. They fundraised for other charities – how might it impact? They decided to express their concerns directly to the parish priest, emphasising the substantial time they had devoted to getting their initiatives off the ground and the services that were dependent on their fundraising. He agreed to bring their concerns to the next Pastoral Council meeting.

The two men who joined were very taken by the council's engagement with this and other matters. Once they found their feet they too participated in the discussions. One of them got involved in assisting the secretary with correspondence and was genuinely disappointed when it became apparent that this was not the right time for the project.

A few months later some foreign nationals came to work for the employer of the other man. He won their trust because, through his Pastoral Council experience, he realised the need to clarify expectations graciously and fairly very early on. His employer, noticing the connection he had established with them, promoted him and his new responsibilities included oversight of these new employees. His faith had led him to be a beneficial presence in the lives of his new colleagues, illuminating a key insight of another spiritual writer, Frederick Buechner, 'Vocation is the place where your deep gladness [helping others] and the world's hunger [immigrants with needs] meet.'[10] Through this experience he also recognised the need to put the integration of foreign nationals on the Parish Pastoral Council agenda. He was also mindful, through past discussions, that many parishioners were likely to need to be supported in getting to know the new people in their midst. ❧

If we were to discuss this story, there are many aspects that each of us could comment upon. I share it because it is profoundly pastoral and deeply rooted in gospel values. How does our parish welcome the stranger? It also speaks of an ongoing experience many active councils face – clarification as to their role at this time.

During the weeks that I wrote this book two departments of the Roman Curia also published resources pertinent to the ministry and continued evolution of Parish Pastoral Councils:

1. On 23 March 2020, Pope Francis approved a new *Directory for Catechesis* prepared by the Pontifical Council for Promoting the New Evangelisation. The Directory provides guidelines for the Church's mission of proclaiming the Gospel through catechesis and evangelisation for the foreseeable future.
2. On 29 June 2020, the solemnity of Ss Peter and Paul, the Congregation for the Clergy published an instruction entitled *Instruction: The Pastoral Conversion of the Parish Community in the Service of the Evangelising Mission of the Church.*

I would like to offer a brief introduction to their content, i.e. as it pertains to the primary purpose of this book: to help Parish

Pastoral Council members identify and achieve a solid self-understanding as disciples of Jesus Christ, one that supports them and their council realise more of their potential.

If we are to serve with integrity, and I believe we all aspire to, then it is important that we do not work out of either a self-limiting or incorrect understanding of the mission of the Parish Pastoral Council.

The long-awaited updated *Directory for Catechesis* reiterates that each of us (baptised Christians) is a missionary called to finding new ways of communicating the faith with zeal and commitment. Mindful that our contemporary context is now one of religious pluralism, it calls on us to grow in such ways as we will be better equipped to enter 'friendly and cordial dialogue' as a means of witnessing to our faith. This, it asserts, will be the key means by which we can promote the Church's missionary impetus going forward. Regarding the work of evangelisation and catechesis, it proposes three major principles of action pertinent to us as individuals, Parish Pastoral Council members and parish communities: witnessing, mercy/charity and dialogue/conversion.[11] It also acknowledges the need for trained faith-filled catechists,[12] emphasising catechists cannot be credible witnesses for the faith if they themselves have not been catechised and formed for this ministry.[13]

This is an important point in an additional way for Pastoral Council members. Here the Magisterium reminds us that there are matters beyond our competencies. The Directory speaks of the work of catechists involving working with graciousness, dedication and integrity, according to a missionary spirituality that assists them to 'avoid the risk of falling into a sterile pastoral over-exertion'.[14] Pondering this, and having worked as a catechist, I am mindful that Parish Pastoral Councils can, however, exercise a support role, particularly in communities where Christianity is misunderstood as a set of doctrines. Over recent years it has been my privilege to undertake a catechetical programme with parents of children presenting for sacraments. For the past two years I have been joined each evening by three members of the Pastoral Council's Parent Support subcommittee. Each evening they greet us (parents and myself) with a cup of coffee and biscuit. They also participate in the programme, offering rich insights from their own experiences. Their presence has completely changed the programme. There is a real sense of the local faith community taking an interest in and supporting parents, and the authority of the Pastoral Council members far exceeds mine.

The Directory also brings 'the family' into focus noting that in the face of new family scenarios we are called to accompany others with closeness, listening and understanding.[15] It notes the capacity of every family to be a space where those being evangelised can live the faith in a simple and spontaneous way, and where children and adults can receive Christian education in a humble and compassionate manner. How though, are they to become reconnected with their parish community, especially in parishes where it is no longer the custom for Catholic Christians to worship together on Sundays? Surely our Pastoral Councils have a discernment role here too? According to the Directory we are to be catholic (universal) in our outreach, our mercy and our embrace. It also calls on us to be welcoming and recognising of the differently-abled, now 'witnesses to the essential truths of human life' and of their families who are deserving of 'respect and admiration.'[16] It notes the presence of migrants in our communities 'far from their homeland' who 'may experience a crisis of faith.'[17] It reminds us that they are to be supported in the fight against prejudices and the serious dangers they may face, such as human trafficking. Mindful of the stark poverty impacting millions it also notes the need for catechesis to educate people about evangelical poverty and the need to foster indignation within our parishes against situations of misery and injustice suffered by the poor.[18]

I'm quite confident most readers will agree but how are we to support others to come into this reflection? Will we leave it to 'Father' through the homily? Are these really matters for Parish Pastoral Councils? Only, in reality, if they strike a chord with members. Then God has someone or group to work with! As with so many potential initiatives much depends on what our priorities are and whether Pastoral Councils or others are open to exercising leadership.

The Directory also proposes that catechesis should be directed towards educating people in the proper use of the digital culture and by way of supporting a profound ecological conversation. Again I believe we are all likely to agree on the need to help young people to distinguish truth and quality amid the culture of the instantaneous. Thankfully many Catholic schools have entered this space but perhaps there could be parish initiatives to consolidate their efforts? I think particularly of the council that approached the Transition Year Coordinator of the local secondary school on hearing that students were working on social justice projects. The conversation led to the students displaying their projects at the back of the church, much to the delight of both the students, older adults in the parish and parish priest. In this way the young people, though they would never use this language, exercised a much valued 'community apostolate' and the Pastoral Council found a new way of bridge-building with a cohort of teenagers visibly absent from the life of the parish as a faith community.

For those of us socialised into a model of Church that considered our parishes in good shape if they possessed a church, a choir, a school, a few Eucharistic Ministers, Ministers of the Word and a parish priest, the increasing emphasis on catechesis can sometimes feel alien. Where this is copper-fastened by a discretionary attitude on the part of a parish priest or reticence on the part of other members to discuss or explore parish catechesis, there is a real danger that our parish as a faith community will be the poorer for our choice. Our identity and sense of belonging as believers will not be deepened and strengthened by chance. Clergy, Pastoral Councils and catechists working together can take strategic steps that honour our calling to transmit the faith to our children.

The above paragraphs, drawing on the new Directory, provoke many questions. In so far as a Pastoral Council is approaching a time of discernment regarding future priorities, it would be good that those most pertinent to the parish be considered. In highlighting them I am not proposing they dominate future agendas but that they be aired and discussed. Given the overall thrust of the Directory and certain specific references to parish communities going forward,[19] I also anticipate that our bishops will encourage us (committed laity and parish priests)[20] to reflect together again on:

1. The strengths and weaknesses of the current catechesis offered to our young people (#239–256) mindful of their social and cultural contexts and the importance of dialogue in all communication (#302).

2. What our own and others' needs are if we are to begin to think in 'a missionary vein' (#303) and adopt 'a missionary mentality' incorporating 'new styles of relating and communicating' (#308).

3. How best to support 'a process of missionary conversion', one likely to contribute to parish renewal and adaptability, such that our parishes remain or return to being 'the Church living in the midst of the homes of her sons and daughters' (#300).[21]

4. How we might play our part in providing experiences of 'real fraternal closeness' and give expression to a 'concrete witness of mercy and tenderness that produces a sense of direction and meaning' for the very life of the city/large town that our parish is part of (#328).

Recently I had the privilege of reflecting on these matters with a priest friend ministering in the USA. I was struck by his optimism and comment, 'This may not be as complicated as some people might think.' He went on to share briefly how a parish in Los Angeles diocese had invested in a 'coffee trolley' and now encouraged people to linger over coffee served in the church grounds after Mass each Sunday during the summer months. Within weeks the parish priest noticed a significant uptake in participation in Sunday Mass and both he, Pastoral Council members and other parishioners were delighted with the post Mass ten-minute window that allowed them to socialise and affirm one another.

It is also fortuitous that the Congregation for the Clergy's instruction, *The Pastoral Conversion of the Parish Community in the Service of the Evangelising Mission of the Church*, has been published at the same time as the new Directory. Here Pope Francis' 2013 assertion is reasserted:

> How necessary Pastoral Councils are! A bishop cannot guide a diocese without Pastoral Councils. A parish priest cannot guide without Pastoral Councils.

The instruction goes on to say that the necessity does not pertain to the administrative or bureaucratic needs of our parish communities. Rather it takes its authority and purpose from our identity as members of the People of God, 'subjects and active protagonists of the Church's evangelising mission' in our own communities. The invitation is to see ourselves as we truly are: members of pilgrim faith communities that belong to God, 'God's people, sheep of the flock', gifted with the Holy Spirit through the sacraments of baptism and confirmation, invited to know, love and service God in this life, and to be happy with him in the next.

In this spirit the instruction re-echoes St Pope Paul VI, who as early as 1966 wrote: 'It is the function of the Pastoral Council to investigate everything pertaining to pastoral activities, to weigh them carefully and to set forth practical conclusions concerning them so as to promote conformity of the life and actions of the People of God with the Gospel.' We must 'effectively represent the community' of which we, as Pastoral Councils, are an expression. Each council, it reminds us, constitutes a specific setting in which women and men, as followers of Christ, are able to exercise 'their right and duty' to express their own thoughts concerning the good of the parish community to the pastors, and to one another. Here we have an acknowledgement of the need for discussion if pastoral matters are to be honoured as they should.

The document also reasserts that the Parish Pastoral Council 'possesses a consultative vote only' in the sense that its proposal must be accepted favourably by the parish priest to become operative and that the parish priest 'is bound to consider the implications of the Pastoral Council attentively, especially if the other members express themselves unanimously, in a process of common discernment'. Extremes, it notes, are to be avoided, and in so far as possible the council is to consist of those who have effective responsibility in the pastoral life of the parish, or who are concretely engaged in it. This, the Congregation asserts, will help to avoid meetings being 'an exchange of abstract ideas that do not take into account the real life of the community, with its resources and problems'.

As a facilitator of Parish Pastoral Council training I have often encountered raised eyebrows on the part of clergy and laity regarding the teaching that a Parish Pastoral Council 'possesses a consultative vote only'. Is this more of the 'Laity, know your place in our (clergy's) Church!' hogwash that has bedevilled poorly informed clergy and laity for generations? Of course not! Such views are rooted in an authoritarianism debunked in chapter six. Interestingly though, it has its equivalent in the Rule of St Benedict. It too does not propose a democratic model of decision-making, but regarding 'important business' requires that after a careful process of consultation, the leader must take and bear responsibility for their decisions.

If you return to the story about the Parish Pastoral Council who explored linking with a parish in the developing world, you will notice how concerned parishioners went directly to the parish priest. They did so because they didn't want to escalate their concern to the status of a community conflict and they understood his commitment to the unity of the parish. Were they opposed to the link? Of course not! Like the Pastoral Council members, they were working through possible ramifications.

When the matter of 'the consultative voice' arises during Pastoral Council training sessions I frequently bring another element of our Church's teaching to the discussion: the principles of subsidiarity and human solidarity as outlined in Catholic social teaching. During these sessions we always agree on the importance of consulting all members of parish communities in so far as decisions are likely to impact upon them. Sometimes our discussions also acknowledge the challenge of remaining open to others' perspectives, especially in situations where we have found it necessary to be quite robust in presenting our own view. We agree that this too can impinge on good decision-making. We don't always agree that the canonical position is the correct one and then, like Pastoral Councils, we find we must agree to disagree! And that is Catholic too!

The Congregation's instruction contains one final point that it would be remiss of me to omit – the possibility that parishes share a Pastoral Council:

> The flexibility of the norm [regarding establishment of Parish Pastoral Councils] permits the adaptation considered apt

for the concrete circumstances, as for example, in the case of multiple parishes entrusted to a single parish priest, or those within pastoral units: it is possible in these cases to establish a single Pastoral Council for several parishes.

I direct this particularly to clergy and parishioners where Parish Pastoral Councils do not exist or where, in the view of the current membership, a collaborative venture with a neighbouring parish or two might more easily lead to Catholic Evangelical initiatives as illuminated in chapter seven. In his Rule, St Benedict devotes a chapter to 'The Procedure for Receiving Members'. The concern, he suggests, must be whether the novice truly seeks God and sows eagerness for the *Opus Dei* (Work of God), for obedience, and for trials. The novices should be clearly told all the hardships and difficulties that will lead to God.

I don't mean to frighten anyone by putting these two points together. They indicate, however, a fundamental matter. If we agree with Pope Francis that Pastoral Councils are necessary and if there are insufficient parishioners willing to serve according to the true spirit of such councils, then perhaps the correct, mature and best response is to open a conversation with the bishop and neighbouring parish(es) around sharing a Pastoral Council? There is no doubt but that this is a ministry for maturing Christians who are well past the first flowerings of conversion and who are also in demand for other forms of service, such as membership of Boards of Management of Catholic schools or Bethany Bereavement Groups. While there are many such people in every parish, if there aren't sufficient numbers available to form a Pastoral Council, then, a shared arrangement with a neighbouring parish is likely to be the better option.

Whatever our view, another danger we must avoid is being so focussed and driven as to fail to recognise God's presence in ourselves, other members and parishioners. It is this attentiveness which gives the Holy Spirit free play, eventually releasing us from our fears and giving us the confidence to joyfully contribute to the mission of the Church. According to Vest we must 'live into our vocation' and that when we do we shall find we have access to an inner authority that is powerful, 'coming from our deep centre where the Holy Spirit is gradually revealing to us who we are meant to be in Christ'.[22]

❧ In recent years we have had the funerals of much loved priests in the Elphin diocese. On one such occasion I walked from the graveyard with Lilian, one of the first Parish Council members I met on coming to work in the diocese. At that time the priest we were now saying farewell to had taken on the role of PP in her parish. For fourteen years they and others, without fuss or fanfare, contributed to a range of parish initiatives, never seeking any recognition or other form of recompense. As I commended her she smiled and said, 'Ah, but we did it for the Lord!' I shouldn't have been surprised. Her words took me back to a question our priest friend explored with me late into a November night, how he and his brother priests might best support Pastoral Council members expand their spiritual horizons as well as attend to important parish matters? This highly experienced and caring pastor had clearly lived with this question for some time. ❧

He understood how busy our heads could legitimately be, that even if we wished to give more of ourselves, we had family, work and other commitments to honour. He knew too that if we were to persevere we would need to be constantly renewed and that from time to time we could well need the satisfaction of feeling our efforts were helping others and appreciated. He noted also, with certain sadness, that there would be those who would never afford themselves the freedom to serve the Church in any meaningful way and that their lives would be the poorer for it. And so his mind and thinking turned to the Master he served and that we serve, and his institution of the Sunday Eucharist.

He was of the view that when we persevere in the faith for a time we come to share St Paul's experience of having an interior yearning to know Christ even better and to share his life with those around us.[23] 'It's like a hunger in us,' he said, 'for something we've tasted and want to taste again and again.' The older I get the more his words resonate. Like St Paul we press on, our interior goal that of possessing Christ more fully as our own. In my case and the case of others who have graciously confided in me, this mysterious hankering brings us to the altar, and to a mystical foretaste of the union awaiting all whom Christ has claimed as his own.[24] Here our offerings, our little oblations, can be gifted with Christ's to the Father in gratitude, praise and adoration. We are also glad to hand over our burdens, and for God to receive them.

Those of us privileged to have received a solid catechesis on the Eucharist are also frequently reminded through our participation of what I term 'the correct order of things'. For example, the Collect[25] on 4 August, the Feast of St John Vianney, patron saint of parish priests, asks God to grant us, 'that through his intercession and example we may in charity win brothers and sisters for Christ and attain with them eternal glory'. We do well to remember that much is dependent on a combination of God's grace and our efforts.

Through our participation in the Eucharist we also have the opportunity to renew the meaning and purpose of our lives in the light of the continued perpetuation of Christ's sacrifice on the cross, death and resurrection (Can. 987). Ideally our parish celebrations will also serve as sacred moments in which we and others reconsecrate ourselves to God. If we have been evangelised and catechised in the Catholic faith it is more likely to be our privilege to intuitively know each Eucharistic celebration as the 'source and summit of the Christian life and the mission of the

Church'.[26] But all of this, attaining this type of understanding, involves a personal commitment to growing into our faith, intellectually and practically.

Another observation I have found to be true is that of Bernadette Gasslein:

> Your community's way of celebrating, will over the years, fashion in people, answers to such basic questions as 'Who is God?', 'What does it mean to be human?', 'What/Who is church?' This characteristic is one of liturgy's most subtle effects: even without noticing it, the ritual activity in which people engage provides them with a theological vision of the world. If well done it will speak the incarnation and paschal mystery more loudly and clearly than any theological discourse. If poorly done, it will fail in this basic mode of strengthening people's faith. Failure to take seriously the two aspects of the nature of liturgy will ultimately impoverish the faith of the people of your community.[27]

It is a salutary passage recognising the Mass as a community responsibility over and above a priest's preserve. Gasslein reminds us of the importance of remaining attentive to how it is celebrated both in and by our communities. Our renewal of the memory of Christ's death and resurrection deserves prominence and we owe a great depth of gratitude to the clergy, altar servers, Ministers of the Word, sacristans, Extraordinary Ministers of the Eucharist, choir members, musical directors, organists, stewards and others who help us to enter it fully, actively and consciously.

There is also a priest in the Elphin diocese who holds the view that the more the service of the altar is respectfully cultivated, the more the business of the Pastoral Council will flourish. Again I perceive a Benedictine connection. Within Benedictine Spirituality there is no dividing line between the holy (the service of the altar) and our other contributions to life and well-being. Among them the service of the altar would lose its spiritual quality if housekeeping, work and community responsibilities were neglected. It's another reason why Parish Liturgy Groups or Pastoral Council Liturgy subcommittees are so important. Our celebrations of the Eucharist remain God's principle means of nourishing every Christian vocation, parish community and humanitarian enterprise. Our councils do well every time they support those who prioritise the planning and preparation of Masses.

Up until recently Eucharistic celebrations were also a key plank of our transmission of our faith. Sadly, the majority of our young people and their parents only join us now on an occasional basis. The fact that parents in particular are consciously or unconsciously opting not to draw upon the spiritual nourishment of the Eucharist has many pastoral as well as catechetical ramifications. For example, it is difficult to comprehend how they will come to recognise themselves as being part of the body of Christ or to feel bonded with it.[28] In recent years I have met many Catholic teenagers committed to holiness of life and open to the mission of the Church, who were surprised to hear that there was an expectation that they would be at Mass on Sundays. Their experience of Catholic community is not parish. It is school or non-existent. I wonder too if we (Pastoral Councils and Catholic School Leadership/Management) would better serve them if we evolved to having an annual joint meeting, when we reviewed together our commitment to their evangelisation and catechesis?[29]

One of our great challenges as local Church today is to connect with the spiritualities of those who see little merit in Church association beyond baptisms and funerals. We are being challenged to evolve a participatory culture which genuinely cherishes people and that honours the essence of Christian Spirituality – the presence of Christ with and for us. When Benedict's Rule was adopted by the twelve monasteries that he helped form prior to moving to Montecassino, the monks knew that they were adopting an alternative rule of life to the one prevalent in the culture and declining civilisation of the time. They, like countless monastic communities over the intervening centuries, were accepting of his encouragement to pursue the spiritual life by first recognising both their dependence on and connectedness with God for the goodness that characterised their existence. Today countless Benedictine women and men testify by their lives to the enduring fruitfulness of this great truth. Like many other Christians they recognise that the goals and values that emerge from so relating with God are quite distinct from those taught by the world around us. Owning, having, consuming, controlling and winnowing are not the high points of the spiritual life. Equally it is not sufficient to seek to be sinless. Rather we must allow ourselves to be directed by God into mission.

When our 'invitations' to become involved in parish and pastoral activities fail to respect the above realisations, it can be difficult for others to see the distinctiveness or goodness of our proposition. Equally people may require time and opportunity to process. Consider for a moment the Church's teaching that parents have primary responsibility for the catechesis of their children in advance of First Holy Communion and Confirmation. Does the Pastoral Council act humbly when it sidesteps a discussion around how best to support them or when it leaves it to the parish priest to make arrangements in the name of the parish?

Parents of faith busy raising children are quite dependent on others for support. Even creating a space that allows them to come together to reflect on their own faith journeys can be a major contribution to faith development in their families. With the assistance of catechists more can be undertaken – and if our parish doesn't have one or doesn't have access to one, perhaps that could also be discussed?

Evolving a participatory culture in parishes is a key and critical challenge for every Pastoral Council. This is especially the case where it has not been the culture for laity to be involved in local Church leadership or where it is still not the culture for committed Catholics to participate in any form of adult religious education enterprise. It's a big challenge, requiring a willingness to re-examine the reality of how we do business and whether in fact we share life. Sometimes the need for change is very apparent, especially when parishes are haemorrhaging. We may need to ask could it be that we are stagnating and that standing still is not an embracement of the mission of the Church? Could part of our challenge be to tackle or combat our own rigidity or fears? Could a key dimension of the challenge of the new evangelisation be the mortification of our self-wills and a move toward a form of spiritual paternity rooted in helping others, such as parents? Have we need of a new communications matrix, one initially more effective than instructive – allowing bonds of Christian community to become established or renewed? Might this be a way Pastoral Councils in partnership with clergy enflesh Jesus' command, 'Love one another as I have loved you? (Jn 13:34)

In my experience, the willingness of women and men to participate in a pastoral project or ministry is contingent on a few things, not least how busy they are. However, personalised invitations accompanied by clarity of purpose, including identification of how their efforts will help others, tend to get a fair hearing. We are much more inclined to take such invitations seriously when the invitation is specific about what we can bring to the project, when we know others are committing and when it connects with our own spiritual compass. In a world where many women and men are under pressure to honour familial and work commitments, it's not surprising that their antennae are only attuned to parish initiatives that speak to their hearts, minds or spiritual needs. Our authenticity with them, as well as with one another, will ultimately derive from our humility. Think of a time when a project was discussed in your presence that did not strike a meaningful chord with you. Contrast it with a time when you had an encounter that engaged you. The latter are indicative of the kinds of spaces we like to enter, as humans, Christians and Parish Pastoral Council members. Membership is not about joining the parish's workhorse or of flogging a dead horse, but of carefully discerning how our limited energy can best be utilised in the service of the Gospel.

According to St Benedict there are four sure pathways to eternal life: obedience,[30] good works,[31] humility[32] and all-embracing love.[33] Parish Pastoral Council service offers opportunities to render all four, and in my experience, this is easier when councils have evolved a culture that values enquiry and dialogue both among themselves and with other parishioners. How have they got there? Goodwill, clarity, good communication, humility and leadership, certainly. Grace and an openness to mission have been equally important. There is always a word of salvation when we are disposed to putting God's will into practice. It's also another reason why we do well to take St Benedict's advice to begin every good work with an earnest prayer to God to bring our good works to perfection.[34]

Notes

1   RB 25:1.
2   RB 24.
3   These pertain to the types of exclusion put forward by Benedict regarding minor and more serious faults. It should not be confused with the kinds of concerns that would have involved excommunication from the universal Church.
4   RB 23:5.
5   RB 30:1–3.
6   RB 24:1.
7   Joan Chittister OSB, *The Rule of St Benedict,* p. 147.
8   Ibid., p. 151.
9   Norvene Vest, *Friend of the Soul: A Benedictine Spirituality of Work*, New York: Cowley Publications, 1997, p. 23.
10 Ibid., p. 25.
11 *Directory for Catechesis*, 31–33, pp. 41–43.
12 Ibid., 110–113, pp. 79–81.
13 Ibid., 130, pp. 91 ff., 425, 242.
14 Ibid., 135 a, pp. 93 ff.
15 Ibid., 226–235, pp. 139–145.
16 Ibid., 269–272, pp. 161–163.
17 Ibid., 273–276, pp. 163–165.
18 Ibid., 279–280, pp. 166–167.
19 Ibid., 240, p. 147; 298–303, pp. 180–183; 308, p. 185; 328, p. 195.
20 Parish priests are re-recognised in the Directory as 'the first catechist in the parish community' (116) but by no means the sole or lone catechist.
21 Here the Directory, quoting Pope Francis' Apostolic Exhortation *Evangelii Gaudium* (The Joy of the Gospel), 2013 (28), and Pope John Paul II's Post-Synodal Apostolic Exhortation *Christifideles Laici* (The Lay Members of Christ's Faithful), 1988 (26), invites us to be sincere in reflecting on the extent to which our parishes are in contact with the homes and the lives of their people, or whether our parishes have 'become a useless structure out of touch with people or a self-absorbed group made up of a chosen few'.
22 Vest, *Friend of the Soul,* pp. 40–41.
23 cf. Phil 3:8, 10:12.
24 cf. Jn 15:15–16.
25 The prayer prayed aloud by the presiding priest before the scripture readings are proclaimed.
26 cf. *Sacrosanctum Concilium* (Constitution on the Sacred Liturgy), 10; *Lumen Gentium* (Dogmatic Constitution on the Church), 11; *Christus Dominus* (Decree on the Pastoral Office of Bishops), 30; *Ad Gentes Divintus* (Decree on the Church's Missionary Activity), 9; *Presbyterorum Ordinis* (Decree on the Life and Ministry of Priests), 5.
27 Bernadette Gasslein, *Preparing and Evaluating Liturgy*, Collegeville: Liturgical Press, 1997, p. 17.

28 cf. 1 Cor 12:25–27.
29 Humility also demands that we question to what extent the exodus away from Eucharist is a consequence of inaction, not on God's part, but ours.
30 RB 5:11; 71:2.
31 RB, Prologue, 17.
32 RB 7:5.
33 RB 72.
34 RB, Prologue, 4.

Chapter Nine

Coming of Age: Where to From Here?

If you uphold me by your promise I shall live;
let my hopes not be in vain.
Sustain me and I shall be saved
and ever observe your statues.

(**Ps 118[119]:116–117**)

Do not be daunted immediately by fear and run away from the road
that leads to salvation. It is bound to be narrow at the outset. But as
we progress in this way of life and in faith, we shall run on the path of
God's commandments, our hearts overflowing with the inexpressible
delight of love.

(**RB, Prologue 48–50**)

This book has been written in a spirit of gratitude. To have regular conversations with women and men – lay, religious and ordained – about God, the Church, parish and family is a great privilege. In every instance our individual spiritualities, personalities and circumstances have coloured our sharing. In some cases we have been happy to share confidences, illuminating our personal struggles. Being people of faith and reason is not without its challenges, particularly when the Lord has bestowed a care for his Church on our hearts. A persistent theme in our conversations has been our individual need to strive for a healthy work–life balance. For most of us, personal prayer is a keystone, a way of processing everything and of returning to an equilibrium that helps us remain upbeat and positive. Among us are those who have come to the realisation that we are at our best when we hand over to God all that challenges our understanding and our goodwill. In our heart of hearts we know God's desire to be intimately connected with us, but a good friend took the wind out of my sails recently when he said, 'but perhaps the real question is "Do we really want to be intimately connected with him?"' It is a question we will return to.

Desiring to give something in return for the trust conferred on me, and mindful of some recurring challenges for Pastoral Council members, I set about writing this book, with a threefold aspiration:

1. To encourage and support fellow lay persons navigating or about to navigate Parish Pastoral Council roles.
2. To offer insight and direction regarding certain universal and prevailing challenges.
3. To introduce a source of inspiration and nourishment (Benedictine Spirituality) that I find helpful.

While I have been writing, the Covid-19 pandemic has impacted on every parish in the world. Throughout this time clergy, other parish personnel and Parish Pastoral Council members across numerous parishes have worked hard, supported by guidance from our bishops and diocesan offices, to facilitate parish celebrations of the Eucharist. Many Pastoral Council members have served as stewards, cleaners and parish social media communications officers. Fellow parishioners have become accustomed to being greeted by women and men on their way into and from Mass and have liked it. Collectively we are grateful for all the individual efforts that have combined to safeguard us from the coronavirus. It has been a trying and stressful time but also one that brought out the best in many of us. We see this too in the innovative outreaches to persons who have experienced bereavements and to vulnerable parishioners. I am mindful also of the Pastoral Councils who have advanced to meeting online so as to be well positioned to discuss emerging pastoral needs. Such meetings are also discussing events such as First Holy Communion and Confirmation celebrations, to the delight of many children. Simultaneously many members recognise that pre-Covid-19 agenda items remain worthy of attention.[1]

As demonstrated in previous chapters, various expressions of the wisdom of the Rule of St Benedict, particularly Benedictine Oblature, offer a useful perspective with regard to reviewing our experiences and aspirations. Pastoral Council members, just like persons with significant corporate and political responsibilities, need to be adept at reviewing the unfolding experiences, needs and hopes of their fellow parishioners. Even with that we need to be committed to acting humbly if we want our contribution to be accepted and valued. The fact that the Gospel is our lens makes little impact unless others, especially fellow parishioners, can see that this is the case. Ours, in this sense, is a sacred work for which we are reliant on God. Equally it is good to appreciate that he is already present to all the situations to which we bring ourselves. We do well, as is our custom, to invoke his blessing during the prayer element of our meetings and to ask for the energy to respond graciously when our energy levels are low.

Thankfully God has many ways of energising us once we turn our gaze in his direction. Principal among them is the celebration of the Eucharist, reflected upon in chapter eight. Many others are encapsulated within our great Christian Spirituality traditions, including Benedictine Spirituality. Here flow streams of encouragement, insight and direction that we can swim in alone or together. Each time we attend to them we attend to God and ourselves.

In chapter one I shared how I came to explore St Benedict's Rule as a means through which to receive, greet and embrace the Gospel. Christ's invitation to each of us to join his mission team now competes with many other voices. As noted, a moment of conversation with a priest friend that centred upon the word 'oblation' in Eucharistic Prayer II, proved pivotal for me. This crystallised something that was in motion for some time, something that has found expression in these pages. Perhaps there is a similar moment or moments in your own faith journey? If there is, I encourage you to attend to it. God being God, such blessings always extend to others, enriching life now and into the future.

Chapter two offered a brief introduction to Benedictine Oblature as something which speaks to the hearts of intentional and maturing Christians across all seven continents today. Readers were also encouraged to see themselves as being among the Lord's chosen workers, and to believe their yearning for fullness of life to be integrally linked to God's invitation to be of service. To trust God's faithful love and constancy is a big step in everyone's faith journey.[2] It's also a personal step that no other person can take for us. Though the scriptures and other sources of revelation tell us God will support us, his intervention always seems to follow our commitment.[3] Once we take the plunge we soon learn that our 'big' step must be followed by other steps. Agreeing to serve on one's Parish Pastoral Council can be one of them. To say yes to membership in a non-presumptuous way opens us to the struggle of working out what we are about. It's a work no one can do for us. Like Jacob we can find ourselves wrestling with God,[4] finding it difficult to either discern or accept his will. Membership can be personally challenging, especially when we anticipate the support of others and it is not forthcoming, or our other responsibilities simultaneously clamour for our attention. What holds many members through the struggle of working out what the council is about is their personal faith and their experience of fellowship through meetings. They stay because their intuition tells them God wants them there. As noted in the opening paragraph we know God's desire to be intimately connected with us, but as my friend noted, the critical question is 'Do we really want to be intimately connected with him?'

The disposition of our hearts and those of fellow members has a huge bearing on a body such as a Parish Pastoral Council. It is the reason why certain councils, despite great difficulties, are persistently life-giving in character. Oftentimes their energy is rooted in the faith commitment of a few members. I love being in their company because they embody a conviction that rests deep in our being, that our Christian faith is meant for sharing. Though they rarely see it in themselves they embody a missionary spirit ever willing to support initiatives that help others grow in faith; for example, sponsoring of young people as assistants to persons with disabilities during their diocese's pilgrimage to Lourdes.

The same disposition is probably present in every council but it is not as evident. At the level of identity we can be loyal to the Church, profess an abiding faith, but never get round to living in a missionary key.

When that spirit prevails, there's a passivity to us that can be followed by a move from regular to infrequent meetings. In playing it safe, we can cease to play at all!

It is for this reason that chapters three, four and five proceeded to focus on three fundamental Benedictine dispositions: *obedientia* (obedience/attentive living), *stabilitas* (stability) and *conversatio morum* (daily attentiveness to conversion of heart, permanently striving to improve one's attitude and participation in community life as an expression of one's desire for union with God). I am convinced that how we see and attend to ourselves spiritually has a huge bearing on our participation in Church life. Few Christians in my experience present themselves as God's gift to humanity and God help them if they should ever opt to do so! But the One who created us in love for love and who sees us as we truly are – eternally loved children of the eternal God – the One who desires to share the divine life with us and who says, 'I have come that you may have life and have it to the full' (Jn 10:10), is he glorified by wilting parishes and dioceses where the overarching movement is away from rather than toward the Church?

Benedictine Spirituality, as chapter three illuminates, places a huge emphasis on *obedientia* as a personal and communal disposition. As noted it is 'about especially good hearing, about learning to listen very attentively'. When we turn the ear of our hearts toward him and follow up on what we hear, God's love comes to fruition in us. What we hear from him we can trust, for his word is always for our good and the good of others, and never a word oriented toward an evil intent or outcome. But as those parenting children know, what is good is not always popular, lauded or immediately accepted. Again we are back to my friend's profound question, 'Do we really want to be intimately connected with him?'

In highlighting *stabilitas*, chapter four illuminated our calling 'to persevere over time, rising and falling and rising again'. This is especially necessary when our interpersonal experiences with others are challenging. One of the perennial dangers for every Parish Pastoral Council is that our communication becomes superficial or so politically correct as to amount to a sham. When this happens, our capacity to exert a positive influence or impact positively in the lives of others is greatly reduced. *Stabilitas* commits us to our Gospel-based values systems, community and commitment such that we can't run or hide from difficulties. Ultimately it supports us in naming and facing issues, always accompanied with the aspiration to make life better for others as well as ourselves.

Some stories were shared highlighting how *stabilitas* can underpin fundamental Christian values such as hospitality,[5] illuminating the practical results it can have at pivotal times of transition in people's lives. Here we encountered encouragement to obey our gut, especially when it tells us 'to dig in', but always in a manner that respects and honours the gifts, insights, responsibilities and generosity of others and, most importantly, the reality of God's presence in everyone.

Stabilitas can also prove significant during times of national debate regarding constitutional matters. I think particularly of meeting Joe, proud dad of Maria who loved participating in the Special Olympics. A majority of Irish voters had just passed the thirty-sixth Amendment of the Constitution of Ireland (2018) permitting the Oireachtas to legislate for abortion. The Irish Constitution had previously prohibited abortion unless there was a serious risk to the life of the mother. Joe, like many others, had been rattled by certain aspects of the preceding debate, especially the devaluation of the lives of persons with disabilities. He was very grateful to his parish's Pastoral Council for not fudging the debate and for having organised a pre-vote 'conversation evening'. Here experts from different fields shared their opinions and the group, about forty parishioners, had opportunities to speak with one another. What had stayed with Joe, and what was most consoling for him at that point, was the sharing of some young parents. They too had been upset by the public debate. He was glad to meet them and they had agreed to meet again.

Chapter five, centring on *conversatio morum,* invited readers to embrace Christianity as a commitment extending beyond one's own personal conversion. Here I proposed that if our parishes are to flourish, then important questions, humbly posed, need to be allowed to impact upon our ways of thinking and acting. Christian mission cannot be reduced to believers being committed to their own transformation in Christ. Ultimately that shows limited regard for our brothers and sisters or the prevailing needs of our communities. God has always invited his disciples to be instruments of transformation in their families, communities and beyond. We see this in the lives of clergy, teachers and many others. As contemporary expressions of Christian outreach Pastoral Councils can also be forces for good, particularly by creating spaces that convey solidarity with parishioners open to growing in faith, hope and love.[6] Outreach to Christian immigrants into our parishes is a very good example.

Conversatio morum also places an onus on Pastoral Council members to be honest with each another, truly humble before God, even at the risk of offending others and their sensibilities. Arriving at such a point, I suggested, marked arrival at a stage of maturity and of a more genuine friendship in faith, one rich in potential but also necessitating elements of risk-management. This is much more in keeping with how Christ wants us to be with one another – if not characteristic of how we already relate with one another.

In chapter six our gaze turned in the direction of leadership and authority, individual and collective. Both, as noted, are key to sustaining fruitful and workable arrangements within Pastoral Councils and between Pastoral Councils and their parish communities. This chapter also communicated the vision underpinning the work of Pastoral Councils as proposed by the Irish Bishops' Conference. We also explored some of the considerations that support good pastoral outcomes, such as nurturing a genuine spirit of co-responsibility between parish priest and council members, the importance of sharing ownership of pastoral priorities with the parish at large, and the importance of remaining both Christ-centred and person-centred. A number of insights also provided illuminating on how one might draw on spiritual traditions, such as Benedictine Spirituality, for guidance and development. For example, the chapter invited everyone to recognise an inner 'authority' we must all honour, something borne of holy conviction informed by personal experience and learning.

Though it does not appear in the text, the phrase, 'It ain't what you do, it's the way that you do it!' could be read into chapter seven, 'Evolving Parish Pastoral Initiatives: Humility as a Core Principle of Evangelical Catholicism'. The chapter began with an exploration of the words and phrase 'humility', 'parish' and 'Evangelical Catholicism', and proceeded to propose and illuminate how humility can become a core principle of Evangelical Catholicism in evolving parish initiatives. The chapter also encouraged attentiveness to 'felt needs' mindful that this is where the energy to see projects through also dwells.

At the beginning of chapter eight we saw that St Benedict was not adverse to exclusionary forms of punishment, by way of helping people who offended against their communities get their life in perspective and start over again with a new heart. We noted the struggle life can be for many people and how the spiritual life is a process requiring time, patience, love, help and care for everyone. With this in mind we looked at our calling to be caring and compassionate human beings, and how this might be reflected through Parish Pastoral Council membership, structures and initiatives. We were supported in examining the latter (structures and initiatives) through points taken from two recent magisterial documents, the new *Directory for Catechesis* prepared by the Pontifical Council for Promoting the New Evangelisation and the Congregation for the Clergy's instruction, *The Pastoral Conversion of the Parish Community in the Service of the Evangelising Mission of the Church*. These included Pope Francis' assertion regarding the necessity of Parish Pastoral Councils going forward and the Congregation's reminder that parishes can also share a Pastoral Council.

A note of caution also received expression via the words: What we must avoid is being so focussed and driven as to fail to recognise God's presence in ourselves, other members and parishioners. It is this attentiveness that gives the Holy Spirit free play, eventually releasing us from our fears and giving us the confidence to joyfully contribute to the mission of the Church.

I also recollected a conversation with a priest who expressed his heartfelt desire to see us all happy and well, and his yearning that we, like him, draw life from our participation in our parish's celebration of the Eucharist. A short testimony followed regarding the Eucharist and a query as to whether Pastoral Councils now need to explore how we (faith communities) are to build relationship between those of us who participate in the Eucharist and those who don't? This in turn lead to some sharing regarding the work of building a participatory culture in our parishes, and of continuing to turn to God for inspiration and help.

Now I would like to share three final commendations from the sphere of Benedictine Spirituality, imminently transferrable to Parish Pastoral Council service and other aspects of all our lives.

Firstly, within a monastic or convent community, when the bell tolls it announces a change, a transition. In some instances the monks or nuns lay aside their work to attend to prayer or to eating or to recreation. They lay it down, knowing they will return to it later, and they begin something else with the same attitude. Thus, in a sense, they are 'never busy', but in a calm, continuing line as it were, able to give everything due attention. This form of attentiveness is now no longer the default position for many people. Nevertheless it can serve Parish Pastoral Council members very well – particularly by way of encouraging us to give of our best during the allotted time and then, quite rightly, reinserting ourselves into family and work life. It is important, however, during the tenure of our service, that the gift of our time and talents not be trammelled by other considerations and responsibilities. This is an important hallmark of genuine generosity, which, when supported by definition of role and good working relations, contributes to the rejuvenation of parishes as communities of faith, frequently in a quiet and dignified way. It also removes the risk that we will race to conclusions that might not prove laudable with time.

Secondly, we do well to remember the One we serve, the One whose greeting to us is always 'grace and peace to you from the One who was, who is and is to come' (Rv 1:4). The primary movement of the spiritual life for each of us is enshrined in God's continuous call to each of us *and our personal response.* God, St

Benedict says quite clearly, is within us to be realised, not outside of us to be stumbled upon. Honouring his presence requires that we concentrate from time to time on nourishing the soul rather than sating our senses and appetites, not because they are bad, but because they fail to encompass the great breath of being human. It is for this reason too that we do well to make a little time for silence each day. Increasingly it is necessary if we are to have contact with the Holy Spirit, without whom our capacity to love cannot optimise. In an era when there is much about contemporary life that drains us, 'alone time' is frequently a prerequisite to true communion. Only in silence can our internal hearing apparatus replenish and become attuned to our Creator. And so replenished we can find ourselves better placed to stimulate the kinds of enquiry and developments that help others to turn to God.

Finally, take heart! St Benedict, at the beginning of his Rule speaks about each monastic community becoming 'a school for the Lord's service'.[7] He continues by requesting his readers not to be daunted by fear and not to run away from the road that leads to salvation. He strongly recommends perseverance, conscious that through our sharing in the sufferings of Christ we shall deserve also to share in his Kingdom.[8] So what then is the key to the door of this school for us as lay people? How are we to access the vitality that helps us be good at school? The Holy Spirit provides many answers in the sacred scriptures, not least Matthew 11:28–30: 'Come to me all you who labour and are overburdened and I will give you rest. Shoulder my yoke and *learn* from me for I am meek and humble of heart, and you will find rest for your souls. Yes, my yoke is easy and my burden light.' Our learning, very strikingly, will lead us to rest! God's principal way of working, both for us and through us, is to draw us with the infinite delight of his love. Yes, as Benedictine Spirituality attests, some discipline is required as we are being summoned to grow and exert leadership. But let that never detract from the realisation that it is this kind of divine love that every Parish Pastoral Council is invited to reflect. To do this our presence will always need to be both gentle and humble (as proposed in chapter seven). We are likely to make mistakes. We may even find ourselves embroiled in an occasional disagreement with a fellow student! No matter. Like St Paul I am quite confident that the One who began a great work in each of us will go on completing it until the day of Jesus Christ comes (Phil 1:6).

> *You will have to suffer only for a little while: the God of all grace who called you to eternal glory in Christ will restore you. He will confirm, strengthen and support you. His power lasts forever and ever. Amen.* (1 Pt 5:10–11)

Notes

1   For example, the renewal of other parish ministries, supporting youth faith development, a local response to the environmental crisis (as suggested in Pope Francis' *Laudato Si'*), autumn/lenten adult faith development programmes, organisation of parish missions and better communication between Pastoral Councils and parish communities.

2   cf. Heb 11:6: 'Now it is impossible to please God without faith, since anyone who comes to him must believe that he exists and rewards those who seek him.'

3   cf. Mt 14:15–21.

4   cf. Gn 32:24–28.

5   RB 53, cf. Mt 25.

6   cf. 1 Cor 13:1–13.

7   RB, Prologue, 45.

8   RB, Prologue, 48, 50.

Select Bibliography

AIM (Alliance for International Monasticism), *English Language Bulletin* (An international periodical at the service of monastic communities in the Benedictine Tradition, translated by Dom Henry Wansbrough), Ampleforth Abbey, York, 1998–2020.

Böckmann OSB, Aquinata, *Expanding Our Hearts in Christ: Perspectives on the Rule of Saint Benedict* (Translated by Matilda Handl OSB and Marianne Burkhard OSB, edited by Marianna Burkhard OSB), Collegeville Minnesota: The Liturgical Press, 2005.

Casey OCSO, Michael, *A Guide to Living in the Truth: Saint Benedict's Teaching on Humility*, Missouri: Liguori, 2001.

Casey OCSO, Michael, *Strangers to the City: Reflections on the Beliefs and Values of the Rule of St Benedict*, Massachusetts: Paraclete Press, 2013.

Chittister OSB, Joan, *The Rule of Benedict: A Spirituality for the 21st Century*, New York: Crossroad, 1992, 2010.

Collins OSB, Gregory, *Meeting Christ in his Mysteries: A Benedictine Vision of the Spiritual Life*, Dublin: Columba Press, 2010.

Congregation for the Clergy, *Instruction: The Pastoral Conversion of the Parish Community in the Service of the Evangelising Mission of the Church*, 2020, http://www.clerus.va/content/dam/clerus/Dox/Istruzione2020/Instruction_EN.pdf

de Waal, Esther, *A Life Giving Way*, London: Geoffrey Chapman, 1995.

de Waal, Esther, *Seeking God: The Way of St Benedict*, Minnesota: The Liturgical Press, 2005.

de Waal, Esther, *Living With Contradiction: Benedictine Wisdom for Everyday Living,* Norwich: Canterbury Press, 2003.

Derkse, Wil, *The Rule Of Benedict For Beginners: Spirituality for Daily Life,* Minnesota: The Liturgical Press, 2003.

Dreher, Rod, *The Benedict Option: A Strategy for Christians in a Post-Christian Nation,* New York: Penguin Random House, 2017.

Ezenwegbu, Stephen I., *The Model of Church as Family of God has Implications for a more Viable Ecclesial Life among the IGBO People of Nigeria: A Dissertation Submitted to the Faculty of Humanities in Candidacy for the Degree of Doctor of Philosophy,* Dublin: Dublin City University (All Hallows College), 2015 (unpublished).

Fry OSB, Timothy, *The Rule of St Benedict in English,* Minnesota: The Liturgical Press, 1982.

Gorham, Stephen, *Going Deeper: A Call to Benedictine Spirituality* (booklet), available via Kindle, 2015.

Harrington, Donal, *Tomorrow's Parish: A Vision and a Path,* Dublin: Columba Books, 2018 (revised edition).

Holdaway OSB, Gervase (ed.), *The Oblate Life,* Norwich: Canterbury Press, 2008.

Hume OSB, Basil, *To Be a Pilgrim: A Spiritual Notebook,* Slough: St Paul Publications, 1984.

Irish Catholic Bishops' Conference, *Living Communion: Vision and Practice for Parish Pastoral Councils Today,* Dublin: Veritas, 2011.

Irish Catholic Bishops Conference, *Share the Good News: National Directory for Catechesis in Ireland,* Dublin: Veritas, 2010.

Kardong OSB, Terrence, *Benedict's Rule: A Translation and Commentary,* Minnesota: Liturgical Press, 1996.

Kardong OSB, Terrence, *Benedict Backwards: Reading the Rule in the Twenty-First Century,* Minnesota: Liturgical Press, 2017.

Longenecker, Dwight, *Listen My Son: St Benedict for Fathers,* Pennsylvania: Morehouse Publishing, 1999.

Lyons, Enda, *Partnership in Parish: A Vision for Parish Life, Mission and Ministry,* Dublin: Columba Press, 1987.

Pennington OCSO, M. Basil, *Listen With Your Heart: Spiritual Living with the Rule of Saint Benedict,* Massachusetts: Paraclete Press, 2007.

Pontifical Council for Promoting the New Evangelisation, *Directory for Catechesis,* Dublin: Veritas, 2020.

Simon, G.A., *Commentary for Benedictine Oblates on the Rule of St Benedict* (Translated from the second French Edition by Leonard J. Doyle, reprinted from the 1950 St John's Abbey Press edition), Idaho: Mediatrix Press, 2016.

Vest, Norvene, *Friend of the Soul: A Benedictine Spirituality of Work,* Plymouth: Cowley Publications, 1997.

Williams, Rowan, *The Way of St Benedict,* London: Bloomsbury, 2020.

Wilson-Hartgrove, Jonathan, *The Wisdom of Stability: Rooting Faith in a Mobile Culture,* Massachusetts: Paraclete Press, 2010.